Dads Bek DADLY

67 Truths, Tears and Triumphs of Modern Fatherhood

Dear Kathy & Ira,
Thanks so much for supporting me!
Love

Edited By
Hogan Hilling & Al Watts

10% of the royalties from this book are being donated to the National At-Home Dad Network, a 501c3 non-profit organization that provides support, education and advocacy for fathers who are the primary caregivers of their children. Learn more at www.AtHomeDad.org and follow them @HomeDadNet.

MOtivational PRESS®
LEADERS IN GLOBAL PUBLISHING

Published by Motivational Press, Inc.
7777 N Wickham Rd, # 12-247
Melbourne, FL 32940
www.MotivationalPress.com

www.DadsBehavingDadly.com
Cover photo by: Rocki Hoops, Rockstarr & Co. Photography
rockstarrandco.com

Manufactured in the United States of America.

ISBN: 978-1-62865-101-0

Cove

A special thanks to these da this book:

Matt Swigart

Tray Chaney

David Kepley (photo credit: http://rockstarrandco.com/

Joseph Fowler

PRAISE FOR
DADS BEHAVING DADLY

"*Dads Behaving Dadly* is an important project. In a time when family structure is falling apart, this book will bring back to life the idea that dads are an integral part of a family and of raising a well-adjusted child."
                    - Jenna Hines, Mom Blogger at http://CallHerHappy.com/

***

"The stories are real and moving and so very powerful. I think it's incredibly brave for these fathers to be vulnerable in sharing with the world the tender moments they experience with their children."
                    - Kim Court, Mom Blogger at www.kimcourt.com

***

"I love it!"
                    - Jordan Thierry, Director, The Black Fatherhood Project

***

"This is a book that every Dad as well as every Mom should read. The stories are enlightening and relevant as they remind us of how dedicated today's dads really are to meeting the challenges of being a Father. It's also a good read for young men to show them there are no limits to how to express your devotion when you start a family. Thanks to Hogan Hilling and Al Watts for compiling such an eclectic group of stories to inspire us all!"
                    - Rosalind Sedacca, Author & Founder of
                      Child-Centered Divorce Network

***

"Hogan inspires me every time I hear him talk about fatherhood! Coming from the media myself, I know if we could get every member of the media to read and take to heart the wonderful messages of Hogan and Al's new book, the image of fathers in our society would suddenly zoom back to the reality... that the overwhelming majority of fathers in our world are dedicated, nurturing and loving examples of our Human Family!"

> - Al Cole from CBS Radio. Host of the syndicated talk show
> "People of Distinction"

***

"Really impressed with the writing and the inspiring stories. Lisa Duggan's perspective at the beginning opens other women's eyes about what they have done or are still doing that affects a father's ability to be a dad."
> - M. Garabedian, mother of two children

***

"I totally agree with your concept of the book. I am a father of 3 and President of our Dad's Club at the Elementary school where each of my children went. I am also a Volunteer Varsity Baseball Coach where my son is going to High School. I think Dads should be recognized all the time rather than once a year on Father's Day and this book is a great way to accomplish that."

> - Paul Elischer

***

"I think it's empowering and important for fathers to read essays written by men like themselves - in situations that are unique, yet universal."
> - Jayne Freeman, Certified Childbirth Educator, www.mamarama.tv

***

"My work is mainly with younger fathers (15-25) as well as my own kids (10 & 5). I am very interested in the book project! It looks really great."
> - Ben Wright, Non-Violent Parent Educator

To all men who try every day to be more "DADLY."

CONTENTS

ACKNOWLEDGMENTS

The first time we met was in a hotel room in Kansas City for the 11th Annual At-Home Dads Convention. We agreed to be roommates to save money since we were both stay-at-home dads on tight budgets. Late into that first night, we told story after story about our kids which usually made us laugh hysterically, even the serious ones. These stories made us better dads. We put this book together so more dads could have a similar experience without the awkward hotel room meeting.

We are immensely humbled by the hundreds of dads who submitted a story for this book. Their courage to publicly share their sincere, honest description of life as a dad was beyond our expectations. Many of the dads had not even shared the feelings expressed in their stories with their spouses, partners or friends. We are eternally grateful for their courage and for their faith and trust in us. We are also grateful to Justin Sachs, CEO of Motivational Press, for going all in with us and publishing this book; Laurie Harper, Hogan's former literary agent, for her priceless advice; Tray Chaney for believing in this book from the get go; Andy Ferguson for convincing us to be roommates; the hundreds of dads we've laughed and cried with at the many annual at-home dads conventions we've attended; and Al's wife Shirley who supported our passion and commitment to write this book.

Hogan would further like to acknowledge the people in his life who supported this book endeavor. Mike Marinoff for encouraging him to follow his passion and not give up on this book project; Marynn Garabedian for her insightful, professional wisdom; Elise Cohen Ho, PhDc, HHP; Jennifer Garner of National Association For Balanced Moms; Tom Patty and John Pietro of SCORE for their marketing guidance; Al Cole, CBS Radio Show Host and Founder of People of Distinction; Stacey Wheeler, Founder of Stepdadding; and Helen Gordon for her loving support and encouragement.

Hogan also needs to give a special "Thank You" to Al Watts. In February 2010, an injury due to a major auto accident and ensuing neck surgery left him temporarily disabled. During his recovery, it was evident he could not move forward with the DADLY book project on his own. He reached out to Al Watts and invited him to be the co-editor. Al graciously accepted. Hogan is eternally grateful for Al's writing skills, work ethic and, more importantly, his commitment and faith in this book.

Al would like to acknowledge his children for making him a much better man and for their extraordinary patience during the book writing process (yes, daddy can play now!); the heaping piles of laundry for giving him much needed breaks; and Hogan for inviting him to share in this exhilarating, anxiety-laced thrill ride and being someone he can look up to.

DEDICATED FATHER

Lyrics by Tray Chaney, Waldorf, MD

A song inspired, in part, by *Dads Behaving Dadly: 67 Truths, Tears and Triumphs of Modern Fatherhood*

(Download the song for FREE at www.DadsBehavingDadly.com)

Verse 1:
Definition of a dedicated father.
I Thank God for the position, it's a true honor.
Lookin' at my son in his eyes
I remember when he first told me give 'em high 5.
Malachi was only 2-years-old,
now he 7, oh Lord I know I must be getting old.
Time flies when you busy on your grind
as a man supporting your family all the time.
Remember when we did the first video,
fatherhood was a masterpiece truly dope,
it gave hope to the fathers all around the globe,
106 & Park was a huge platform.
Motivating fathers all over the place,
fist in the air. Fatherhood. Celebrate.
Motivating fathers all over the place,
fist in the air. Fatherhood. Celebrate.

HOOK
Dedicate. Celebrate. Fatherhood celebrate.
All the real men/fathers can only relate.
Each and everyday on your grind
providing for ya family at the drop of a dime!

Salute to my fellas who doing better,
we can make it through the storm no matter the weather.
Take a second, think about it like this,
being there for ya kid, we really makes a difference.

Verse 2
Thinking back when I first met your mother,
you was 8-years-old, just a lil' munchkin.
We use to have conversations 'bout reality,
you told me you ain't really know your real daddy.
You may have seen 'em like 4 or 5 times,
I could tell you was hurt from the tears in your eyes.
I'm thinking, how could a man leave his lil' girl,
then I started reflecting we living in a crazy world.
I don't care what you and the mother went through,
bottom line step up, your kid needs you!
I couldn't sit back and dwell upon the negative,
so I had to make the situation turn positive.
As I took your mother's hand in marriage,
I made a vow to you, don't ever call me your step-parent.
You are mine and I'm gonna make you shine,
fast forward you grow now, again time flies.
I was there for your prom and your graduation,
moments in your life made me such a proud parent.
The point I'm tryna make with the story I'm sharing,
father to a father lets go make a difference!

3rd Verse/Bridge
I'm a man, I'm a father, I'm a husband,
motivating the fathers to keep hustling.
Keep grinding,
keep shining,
set examples for the families worldwide.
Even if we face trials and errors,
get on your knees, pray to God to deliver us.
This is a moment, of celebration. Fatherhood. Dedication!

FORWARD

Lisa Duggan, South Orange, NJ

In the summer of 2005, my daughter was two and a half years old and I had spent the roughly nine hundred and twelve days of her life tethered to her — nursing, changing her diapers or rocking her to sleep. I "stayed home" and my husband went to work. He would take over in the evenings, giving her a bath and putting her to bed.

Most days, we were both pretty happy with our choices. Most days.

On this particular August day, she would not stop crying no matter what I did and I waited anxiously for his call from the train station. Thank goodness it was a summer and a Friday. With his office closing at 1pm, he could be home as early as three. The phone rang but he didn't have good news for me. Instead he had a question: Would it be okay if he stayed in town and went to see a movie?

The Hulk was playing that afternoon and my husband is a huge comic book fan. He had rarely, in those nine hundred and twelve days, missed an evening with his daughter. He worked very hard for us. He never had an afternoon off. I said yes and in that moment, I meant it. Unfortunately, barely fifteen minutes later, I regretted my generosity as the baby continued to fuss. So, I called his cell phone. Was it too late? Had he bought his ticket yet? Please come home.

Of course, there was no reception inside the theatre. I knew, however, that he was deliberately ignoring my calls. I absolutely knew it. My rage grew with each unanswered phone message and I hit redial over and over. By the time hubby emerged from the dark coolness into the hot afternoon sun, there were a half dozen frantic messages on his phone, the last one of our daughter screaming in the background, punctuated by a single, angry sentence from me: "I hope you enjoyed the movie, a—hole!"

The Hulk Incident, as we began to call it, was a turning point in our marriage. It forced us to sit down and re-examine the way we split childcare duties. More importantly, it forced us to examine the unspoken beliefs and expectations we held about one another as a woman and a man. Pre-baby, our life had been pretty equitable. We earned similar salaries and, together, we shared all the domestic chores. How had we become the stereotypical shrieking wife and insensitive husband?

I came to realize that I believed, by virtue of my sex, that only I possessed the innate, nurturing skills necessary to care for our daughter and my husband merely had to show up on time and follow my typed-out instructions. The wider culture reinforced these stereotypes, as did our families. Combine these internal and external prejudices with the high stakes of keeping a baby alive and you have one wary mother. I simply did not believe he could respond to her needs with the urgency required.

At the core of this bias was the notion that men don't need or value love, connection or nurturing in the same quantities as women and, therefore, they are insensitive to those needs in others. However deeply hidden I thought my bias was, my husband was getting the message loud and clear. "You never leave her with me for more than three hours," he said. When I pushed back, he pushed back harder. He reminded me of my early ineptitude at breastfeeding, how I resented her need to be held constantly, how I would often forget diapers or wipes, how I cut her little fingertips when I trimmed her nails.

He asked me if I honestly thought I was as competent or compassionate in those first nine days as I was now at the nine hundred mark and if I believed he loved our daughter any less than me. He helped me to see I wasn't born knowing how to care for a baby, but I had profited from hours of on-the-job training. Now, he was asking for the same opportunity.

We decided the only way to break this dynamic was for me to get out of his way. Way out - like a plane ride away - to see my friend in Chicago for the weekend. By traveling that far, I eliminated the possibility of being able to rush in and rescue them. Yes, I was terrified. Yes, I left lists. And yes, she did end up in the emergency room but not due to any incompetence on his part but to her first bout with croup. I returned from my trip with a new respect for my husband. My daughter had forged a deeper bond with her dad and he had a great story to tell about a frantic car ride in the cold with the windows wide open and balloons made from surgical gloves.

The stories in Dads Behaving DADLY span the ordinary to the extraordinary; they are snapshots of a day in the life of a dad. They demonstrate the wide range of emotions that parenting inspires and show how men experience those feelings equally alongside their mom-counterparts, but in ways unique to dads. There are heartbreaking tales of loss, terrifying plunges into chilly waters and uplifting anecdotes of the miraculous kind. There are epiphanies about work and life and stories of dads who grew closer to their kids by sharing deeply of themselves. These stories aptly relate the confluence of love and pride, horror and exhaustion that comes with the active participation in growing little human beings.

Cultural change, like parenting, is slow and includes much unheralded behind-the-scenes efforts. By the time I saw stay-at-home dads in the news, there had already been sixteen Annual At-Home Dad Conventions. According to the 2011 US Census, "Among fathers with a wife in the workforce, 32 percent were a regular source of care for their children under age fifteen." That's up from 26 percent in 2010. All the research points to the benefits for children and families of an actively, emotionally engaged dad - whether he works full-time, part-time or stays at home. This book documents the benefits of that engagement for the dads.

What's exciting to me about this new fatherhood culture is the opportunity for moms to cheerlead the change but not lead it. The liberation of men and dads is not another task on mom's endless to-do list; dads are not waiting for us to become more actively involved with raising their children. They are taking the reins. Our part is in recognizing when we engage in "gatekeeping" or holding the keys to caring for our kids.

There are so many Mommy-and-Me classes, but maybe moms need a class about dads; one that teaches us the importance of providing ample opportunities, early and often, for dads to care for their kids. Classes that celebrate dads, emphasize their unique value, and teach moms skills for supporting and encouraging a dad's involvement. A dad is not a replacement for mom. Your spouse or partner may parent differently than you, but it's not wrong. Embracing those differences strengthens your partnership. By providing dads opportunities to spend time alone with their children, we help moms, and more importantly, we help our kids by ensuring they have two, capable and confidant caregivers.

Parents are dependent upon each other to make mutually beneficial choices in dividing the work of care-giving. We all labor under the long held prejudice that says men are not programmed for nurturing. It's tempting to retreat into rigid stereotypes for men and women when we're scared or unsure of our own abilities. Together, we can prepare for this internal bias, and work together to be conscious of its influence on our expectations for our husbands and partners — and ourselves. For me, there is great comfort in knowing I have an equal partner for this undeniably tough, but joyous, work.

Stories like the ones in this book will help open our minds and hearts to the reality that men can — and do — parent as well as any woman.

INTRODUCTION

Al Watts, South Elgin, IL

I wasn't sure I could be a good dad. I had no experience with babies and the few times I babysat some neighborhood boys, it was pretty much a disaster.

After labor with our first daughter dragged on for 26 hours, my wife was finally wheeled into the operating room for a C-section. The procedure took only a few minutes but after the long labor, my wife was exhausted. She kissed our new baby on the head and was wheeled to recovery.

I was alone. And my daughter started to scream.

I had counted on my wife to tell me what to do but she wasn't there. I could have asked the nurses for help except I knew my wife was counting on me to be there for our little girl.

Somehow I remembered from a birthing class we attended that babies instinctively like to suck. I stuck the ring finger of my right hand into our daughter's mouth and she instantly quieted down. For 2 hours, the only thing that kept her happy was sucking on my finger. In that moment, I realized I could be a good dad.

Forty years ago, this intimate father/daughter moment would not have happened. Most dads weren't allowed in the delivery room or believed soothing their baby was part of their role. A dad's role was to provide financially for the family, offer stern discipline when necessary, and enjoy his children in whatever spare time he had. This remains the perception by many in society about what dads still want today.

It isn't.

More and more fathers are asserting themselves, actively taking part in changing diapers, attending doctor's appointments, participating in PTA meetings and helping with homework. Increasingly, men like me have chosen to leave the workforce to be stay-at-home dads. The mold of father as only a breadwinner is breaking. The result is a new fatherhood culture and it is changing the very definition of what it means to be a dad.

In the following pages, dads of different socio-economic backgrounds, races, and family structures candidly describe the truths, tears and triumphs of modern fatherhood. Their honest, heart-warming, heart-breaking and humorous messages provide an in-depth look into how fatherhood has changed and how men are handling the more active parenting role they now want. They are "dads behaving DADLY".

A new image of fatherhood will emerge as you read these stories. No longer will you see dads as stoic, inept, incompetent, hands-off parents. You will see dads are in the trenches; changing diapers, teaching independence and sacrificing career advancement to do what it takes to be involved parents. You will learn how dads parent differently and how it provides unique benefits for their children.

To understand how and why dads are becoming more actively engaged parents, it is important to understand a little of the history of fatherhood. Before the dawn of the industrial age in the 19th century, nearly every family in the U.S. lived on a subsistence farm or was engaged in a specific trade such as cobbler or blacksmith from their home. Gender roles were more loosely defined, meaning moms and dads shared some of the financial, domestic and child care duties.[1]

When the industrial age began changing the way goods were produced and how farms operated, it also pushed moms and dads into definitive gender roles. Dads began leaving home for work in warehouses, factories, and shipyards or ran cash crop farms. Many of the domestic activities such as making clothes or candles became items purchased instead of made at home. This meant mothers were able to focus more time on their children and managing the household while fathers increasingly were able to earn enough money to support the family. Mothers also began to be seen as more capable of shaping the character of their children than fathers since they stayed home and away from the "corrupting influence of business and politics."[2]

[1] Mintz, Steven. Mothers and Fathers in America: Looking Backward, Looking Forward http://www.digitalhistory.uh.edu/historyonline/mothersfathers.cfm
[2] Mintz, Steven & Kellogg, Susan (1988). *Domestic revolutions: a social history of American family life*, xviii, xix

Progressive era reforms of the early 20th century and the idea of the "family wage" championed by Henry Ford made it possible for most men in every class to be able to earn enough money to fully support the family on their income alone. Masculinity became tied directly to work. Childcare and domestic duties became exclusively feminine.[3]

Family dynamics began to change with the women's movement in the latter half of the 20th century. Women wanted more opportunities. They went to college, obtained jobs, and demanded equality in the workplace. Women wanted to be defined by more than just motherhood and they began achieving it.

Today, women make up half of the workforce. They earn the majority of college degrees, which provide them with better opportunities for good-paying, stable jobs.[4] Wives often contribute significantly to the household income of married families with nearly 35% of them earning more than their husbands.[5]

Until women were able to make a significant economic contribution to the family, dads had to work. Now dads have opportunities and choices they never had before, making modern fatherhood possible. "The movement of married women into the labor force," explains the Census in its latest report on child care arrangements, "has changed the organization of daily life and has allowed fathers to be more available for child care while their wives are working."[6]

Gradually, but quietly, more and more dads are sharing household and childcare duties with moms. The amount of time dads spent caring for their children has tripled in the last 30 years and is nearing the average

---

[3] Mintz, Steven. Mothers and Fathers in America: Looking Backward, Looking Forward http://www.digitalhistory.uh.edu/historyonline/mothersfathers.cfm

[4] Fry, Richard, Cohn, D'Vera, Pew Research Center (2010). New economics of marriage: the rise of wives, http://apewresearch.org/pubs/1466/economics-marriage-rise-of-wives

[5] Bureau of Labor Statistics, "Table 25: Wives Who Earn More Than Their Husbands, 1987-2008," Women in the Labor Force: A Databook: 2010 (2010).

[6] Laughlin, Lynda, U.S. Census (2010) Who's minding the kids? Child care arrangements spring 2005/summer 2006 15

time of moms.[7] According to a survey conducted by Yahoo in 2011, fifty-one percent of men are the primary grocery shopper in the family.[8] Thirty-two percent, according to the Census, are the primary caregiver.[9]

While the opportunity for financial stability without entirely depending on dad opened the door for change, it is not the sole reason for it. Dads have, in most cases, embraced this freedom and are doing what they really want to do: be more involved with their kids.

Many people still believe a man's primary role is that of breadwinner in the same way they used to believe a woman's primary role was that of the primary caregiver. Over the last 50 years, women have shown they are capable of being much more than primary caregivers. Men are now showing they are capable of being much more than a breadwinner.

Recent research shows dads are biologically capable of nurturing, have a desire to share child care duties with their wives, and that active involvement in parenting by fathers improves the lives of their children. A study by Dr. Svend Madsen of Copenhagen University found babies are equally capable of attaching to men as women and "fathers can be just as loving, caring and effective parents as mothers."[10] Lee Gettler of Northwestern University and his colleagues found that men are affected biologically when they become dads because testosterone levels decrease when men become fathers.[11] A study of working dads by the Boston College Center for Work & Family found that dads "were

---

[7] Konigsberg, Ruth Davis (August 8, 2011). Chore Wars, *Time Magazine http://www. time.com/time/magazine/article/0,9171,2084582,00.html*

[8] Neff, Jack (2011). Time to rethink your message: now the cart belongs to daddy, *Advertising Age*, http://adage.com/article/news/men-main-grocery-shoppers-complain-ads/148252/

[9] U.S. Census Press Release (2011). One-third of fathers with working wives regularly care for their children. http://www.census.gov/newsroom/releases/archives/children/cb11-198.html

[10] Madsen, Sven Aage (2007). Men too are competent caregivers, European Fatherhood, http://european-fatherhood.com/knowledge.php?mode=view&id=49

[11] Gettler, Lee T., McDade, Thomas W., Feranil, Alan B., & Kuzawa, Christopher W. (2011). Longitudinal evidence that fatherhood decreases testosterone in human males, *Proceedings of the National Academy of Sciences*, doi: 10.1073/pnas.1105403108

deeply committed to care-giving and sharing the work evenly with their spouses."[12] Child Psychologist Dr. Kyle Pruett of Yale has found through his extensive research on dads that an involved father decreases poverty, drug abuse, and teen pregnancy in their children.[13]

Many dads, however, are still afraid to be the fathers they want to be. Movies, TV shows and news articles often depict dads as inept and incompetent when it comes to basic childcare. These images convince many dads they would fail so they refrain from active participation as parents. From our personal experiences as stay-at-home dads and the thousands of dads we have met, we have seen how well dads can succeed as caregivers.

Hogan began leading workshops for fathers at local hospitals in 1994. He heard powerful stories of doubt, excitement, and joy; the truths about modern fatherhood dads were afraid to tell anyone outside of that room. They feared no one would really listen to them or they would be considered less of a man for expressing their true feelings. Through other workshops, community events and fatherhood networks Hogan has participated in, and the numerous Annual At-Home Dads Conventions both of us have attended, we have heard more and more amazing and inspiring moments of dads behaving DADLY.

The truths, tears and triumphs dads have shared with us about their real life experiences are far different from what most people have seen in the media. The dads we have met expressed emotions and achievements few would believe a dad would reveal. It is what has kept us so passionate about advocating for involved fatherhood and why we were compelled to assemble their messages into this narrative about modern fatherhood.

In the following pages, real, honest, sincere, devoted, and caring dads share the successes and challenges of modern fatherhood. Their stories represent not only all that is good about fatherhood but candidly convey how real dads feel about being a dad.

[12] Harrington, Brad, Van Deusen, Fred, Ladge, Jamie (2010). The new dad: exploring fatherhood in a career context 28 http://www.bc.edu/content/dam/files/centers/cwf/pdf/BCCWF_Fatherhood_Study_The_New_Dad1.pdf

[13] Pruett, Kyle D. (2000). Fatherneed: why father care is as essential as mother care for your child

We encouraged dads to not hold back, pour their hearts out, and write personal narratives about life as a good father. The response was overwhelming and far exceeded our expectations. The 67 truths, tears and triumphs you will read will not only surprise and inspire you but will completely change what you thought you knew about dads.

PART ONE

I AM YOUR FATHER

"It was terrifying to know I was responsible
for another life."
- *Tirono Hill, father of one son in Winnsboro, SC*

DAD TO BE OR NOT TO BE

Tray Chaney, Waldorf, MD

I had been in Las Vegas for a couple days in February of 2005 attending "The Magic Show", an event where individuals in the entertainment industry come to showcase some of the hottest fashion items: clothes, shoes etc. As the actor who played the character "Poot" from one of the most powerful and influential shows of all time, "The Wire" on HBO, I was highlighted as one of the featured models/spokespersons for one of the popular clothing lines. Everywhere I went, I heard: "Hey Poot!" Each warm welcome brought a smile to my face that made me realize how lucky I was to receive the heart-warming accolades. But I was also smiling and felt fortunate for another reason my fans didn't know. I was about to become a dad.

As much as I was enjoying the event, I was anxious to return home to Washington, DC to hear my wife tell me the sex of our new baby. She was to have the ultrasound while I was in Vegas.

When I arrived home, I kissed Ayesha, who was five months pregnant. I rubbed her stomach like I always did since I received news we were expecting. I couldn't wait any longer so I popped the big question. "So honey, is it a boy or a girl?"

Ayesha recommended I take a seat on the bed and said, "Tray, I need you to brace yourself!"

Now I'm thinking, "OMG, we are having twins!!" and I could barely contain myself. Then I realized she was not smiling. With a heavy heart, she delivered the sad news.

"Tray, I went to the doctor yesterday and the baby doesn't have a heartbeat."

"Huh?" I couldn't really register what she had said. My mind went blank. Or maybe I knew what she said but didn't want to accept it.

As I sat there in disbelief, I asked Ayesha to repeat what she said.

BECOMING DAD

Vincent Daly, New Rochelle, NY

"Honey, I am pregnant."

The days and months following those four words rushed by like a cascading effect, knocking down my previously held priorities and erecting new ones. The deconstruction of the lifestyle I once dearly held as a husband, ran parallel to the construction of the new man I was to become. My fiercely independent self would need to adapt or get crushed by the reality of bringing a human being into this world. Stress-laden thoughts, sleepless nights, irrational fears and more could all be attributed to the enormous change I, as an expectant father, had to attempt to grasp in a small window of time.

I remember often hearing from my family members and friends with children how I should "enjoy myself" now because, once our child arrives, everything about my life would change. We were told the freedoms my wife and I enjoyed and took for granted would no longer avail themselves to us as parents. They were not trying to be vindictive. They were preparing me for my new life as a dad and family man.

To say I was in crisis mode throughout our pregnancy would be a drastic understatement. Struggling with this new identity of being a dad coupled with an increasing sense of uncertainty about my parenting abilities consumed me. I didn't feel I'd ever be ready. I was a man overwhelmed with the huge responsibility of fatherhood. I was also buried neck-deep in self-doubt with questions no one could answer with the tide rising. Emotionally, I became unhinged without a means to reconnect. The comforting words from relatives and friends fell on deaf ears. Debilitating stress formed a nearly impenetrable wall.

As our due date approached, my anxiety heightened further. When my wife and I attended Lamaze classes, my heartbeat would often drown out the sounds in the room.

During my wife's pregnancy, I expressed how I was adamantly opposed to being in the delivery room for the birth of our son. "Just too much for me to handle!" I lamented.

I found myself lost in thought about my competence as a future father. But then I experienced a Zen meditation mantra – "our child will be what saves me." The thought of our child "saving" me gave me a sense of calm and the one clear connection which enabled me to brush aside the mountain of thoughts weighing heavily on my mind.

Just when I thought I had some sense of control over my anxiety, our son decided to arrive two weeks early. From the moment we left the house for the hospital, everything was a blur. Despite my reservations and anxiety about witnessing our son's birth, I followed my wife into the delivery room. I comforted her as she endured excruciating pain like a champion. The nurse rushed in and instructed me to hold my wife's leg. Moments later I was officially a Daddy. Suddenly my anxiety was replaced with awe.

After the nurse had cleaned up our son, she asked if I'd like to hold my son. I almost unconsciously replied to her, "no, that's okay" because quite frankly, I had never held a newborn baby, let alone my own. Although the nurse understood my anxiety, she smiled and handed my son to me. As I held him in my arms, I stared for what seemed like hours at this little life before me.

Six years later I'm now the father of two beautiful children. The joy and challenges of fatherhood continue to evolve as they grow and so does the context of what it means to be a father. As a whole, today's modern dads have made the conscious decision to be more engaged in the lives of their children. Collectively, my fellow dads and I are navigating unchartered waters. Yet that's okay. No one ever said this new and wonderful evolution of fatherhood would be easy.

AM I READY?

Scott Cathcart, Wesley Chapel, FL

The day began early with a trip to the hospital at 6:30 a.m. for our scheduled induction. Madison Rose was two days past her due date and she apparently had no intention of coming out; she was enjoying her "mommy hot tub." Once we were checked in, we tried to settle down for our first experience as parents-to-be.

The morning ran into afternoon and eventually into evening as my wife slowly dilated. Finally the time was near. I had spent the last couple of months wondering, sometimes aloud and sometimes to myself, whether or not I would "make the grade" as a father. I was excited to be a dad, but also nervous and unsure about my first interaction with my baby girl.

At one point during the pregnancy, I made up a song I sang to my wife's belly for Madi. It became a daily ritual before I would go off to work and as soon as I came through the door in the evening. I also talked to her quite a bit to make sure she knew my voice, although I wasn't completely sold on the fact she could actually hear me.

It was now time to push, and very soon, I would officially be a dad. How would I do? Would I be awkward holding her? Would I drop her? Would her head fall off if I didn't support it properly? I didn't particularly like babies, and had no siblings growing up, so I didn't have much practice at taking care of little bundles of joy.

Then it finally happened. Madison Rose came into the world on August 29, 2003, a little after 6:30 p.m., almost 12 hours after we arrived at the hospital.

The doctor and nurse took Madi and placed her on the weighing table to get her height and weight. Her little lungs were working just fine… she was belting out some nice melodies!

With my trusty video camera in hand, I approached her slowly and began talking out loud to her as she was crying. That's when the most

the cookies are oval instead of round. Sometimes the cookies come out broken. What matters most is the right ingredients.

I came out of my stupor and grabbed my wife's leg with the authority of a seasoned nurse. I encouraged my wife to breath and push along with the other nurses and, before long, out came my son.

After that, I knew none of my plans would come to fruition. The birth of this kid had rocked my center and I have been learning lessons from him ever since. He has taught me to be open to anything, how to love better and have a deeper more genuine joy about life. All I had thought was reality was now a fantasy; he changed my perspective with his first breath and I took mine as a new person.

I would never again be who I was. I was a dad now and had a new identity, new responsibilities. My breaths were deeper and my perspective clearer. My realities were now about bandaged knees and temper tantrums in the middle of Disney World. This is what my sum total was always supposed to equal.

Rohen is now 3 and if I tried to articulate to him about my "moment" now, he would probably just crinkle his brow and say "huh?" So until the day comes when I can tell him about his impact on me and have him understand, I will bait a 1,000 hooks, I will throw 10,000 balls, I will tuck-in 1 million times. Still, even then he will never know - just as I didn't know - how insufficient the word "love" is in describing how much he means to me.

SPECIAL DELIVERY

Matt Swigart, Cottage Grove, MN

It was July 28, 2010. The night before, I had just returned from leading a mission trip to Panama for sixteen days. When we found out we were pregnant, we knew this mission trip was very close to our due date. It was important to me and my work so we decided to risk me making it back in time for the birth. Little did we know how big of a risk our decision would be.

The day started out the same as every other typical post-mission trip day. I rested, ate my favorite foods cooked by my wife, and listened to all the things our other two children had been doing while I was away. My wife, meanwhile, was having some contractions which we both knew was fairly common the closer we came to her due date. As the day went on, however, her contractions became more intense. It was time to start getting ready to go to the hospital.

We called my in-laws to take the other kids to their house so we could leave. They arrived and helped me gather up all their things. As I was getting the kids out the door, I heard my wife yell, "Oh! My water just broke!"

With our first two children, we had about ninety minutes after my wife's water broke before the baby was born. So, when my wife's water broke this time, I wasn't worried. We still had plenty of time to get to the hospital.

"OH! I need to push!"

"NOOO!" my brain screamed. "We're still at home!"

I dashed upstairs, got a towel and brought it down to my wife. She was already on the phone with her midwife who told her to call 9-1-1. There wasn't time to make it to the hospital. I went back upstairs to get my shoes on just in case we needed to make a mad dash for it and I quickly dialed 9-1-1.

"Matt, I can see the head!" yelled my mother-in-law. I immediately went into superhero mode, flew down the stairs and around the couch. My wife was lying on the floor with the top of my daughter's head sticking outside of her. Without thinking, I reached down, grabbed my daughter by the head and pulled her out!

I was in shock. I was thrilled. I felt like I was going to throw up and fill my pants at the same time. My hands had just delivered my own baby!

Who's the man?!?!

I sat there, in awe, with our daughter in my arms. She was struggling to breathe because, normally when a baby is forcefully pushed out, the mucus in their lungs and throat is also pushed out. Well, little Lucy Fayth didn't have the pleasure of being forcefully pushed out. Her breathing sounded like Rice Krispies when you pour milk on it. Thankfully we still had the 9-1-1 operator on the line. The operator told me what to do to help get her airway clear while we waited for the paramedics.

Finally, about four to five anxious minutes later, the paramedics showed up and sprang into action. They suctioned her nose and mouth and we saw normal color come to her skin. Once she started breathing well, she just sat there quietly looking around. I imagined her thinking, "What just happened?"

An hour later, after the doctor checked out Lucy and my wife in our hospital room, I went for a short walk to come to grips with what had just happened. All at once I was flooded with emotion. Coming off the mission trip experience and then going through this exhilarating birth, I literally lost it. I was never much of a crier but having children, especially daughters, has softened me completely. I wept harder than I ever had before, not out of sadness, but out of gratitude that God would find me worthy of being used by him around the world and in my home to serve my wife and raise my children. It is incredibly humbling to be entrusted with the care of lives and, never more than in the moment I brought life into this world, was I more aware and blessed.

NURSING THE LETDOWN

Andy Goldstein, Pegram, TN

Here's the thing about breastfeeding that you will not read in any book: it's not as easy as it looks, and for some moms, it's just not going to happen.

Lactation specialists make it look easy, and the moms who can breastfeed their children in the middle of packed shopping malls make it look easy, but for my wife and I, breastfeeding just wasn't in the cards.

It's not that the desire wasn't there. It absolutely was. I was a breastfed baby and turned out absolutely perfect by my own standards. Though my wife was not breastfed (but still turned out perfect), she knew right away she wanted to have that connection and bond with our baby. I wholeheartedly supported this decision and immediately began gathering all the essentials she would need to make it happen for us: breast pump, breast pads, breast milk storage bags, Boppy pillow, Lanolin, etc.

We both read copious quantities of books and Internet articles about breastfeeding. In fact, it's the most literature I'd consumed featuring breasts since I got my hands on the Katarina Witt *Playboy* in my teenage years. My wife and I became versed on such ideas as the benefits of colostrum and how to tell apart a good latch from a bad one.

We even signed up for a lactation course at the hospital. I wasn't about to miss this opportunity to not only learn more about something so vital to our family, but to be there to support my wife, as well. Most of the women in the class had men with them, but some didn't. I couldn't help but feel bad for the moms who were alone. Not for any spiritual or deep reason, but because it's much more fun to breastfeed a Cabbage Patch Kid in the football hold when someone close to you is there to offer both encouragement and well-timed jokes.

We had the knowledge. We had the gear. My wife had the breasts. I had the male support locked and loaded. We were ready to embark on the yearlong breastfeeding journey.

When our son, Evan, was born a little after 2 a.m., we were both quite tired, but my wife was still excited to begin the first feeding. Unfortunately, we hit a snag.

Though my wife was clearly producing enough milk (she looked like one of the buxom women I saw in the *Playboy* I referenced earlier), it wasn't coming out in the streams we thought it would. The nurses and lactation specialists told us it was okay. As long as she kept trying, Evan would get enough colostrum, and he would be fine.

Deep down, we knew something was wrong. An hour's worth of pumping would yield less than one ounce. We watched videos on YouTube showing breastfeeding mothers shooting milk like John Wayne with a Colt revolver. We remembered the episode of *Roseanne* where Jackie leaked through her shirt when her baby started crying. My wife didn't have the same experience.

After a few more days of trying, Evan began to show jaundice. It was becoming clear he was not getting enough milk. My wife went back to see the same nurse who taught our lactation course. The nurse confirmed what my wife already knew: her letdown reflex was non-existent, and we needed to either supplement formula while continuing to try to breastfeed or go with formula full-time. We went with the latter.

It was crushing to my wife, and heartbreaking for her milk to dry up. We felt relieved Evan took to the formula, but she still felt defeated. She felt like she let us all down.

Through all this, I did what any good husband would, and should, do. I tried to assure her it wasn't her fault. She wasn't the physical freak show she thought she was because she couldn't expel milk. I tried to make sure she knew I wasn't disappointed Evan was going to be formula fed. I told her on multiple occasions I didn't think formula was going to stunt his physical and mental development compared to babies chowing down on breast milk. I told her the extra expense of buying formula did not matter, and was nothing to lose sleep over.

But most of all, I told her she was an amazing mother, and Evan and I were lucky to have her.

I COULDN'T PROTECT THEM

Joseph Fowler, Bloomington, IN

The C-section for our second child was scheduled for 9 am on a sunny, warm day on May 17, 2011. Arriving on time to the hospital was the only thing that went according to our plan.

I was very excited about the upcoming birth of our second child. The birth of our daughter two years earlier made us a family. This child was going to complete it. I couldn't wait to fit this final piece of the puzzle neatly into the place of my increasingly perfect life.

Everything started out just as it did when we had our first, except I was much more relaxed. I had been here. I had done this before. I was ready to meet our child.

We were in the operating room and the doctor carefully opened my wife up. We thought everything would happen very quickly as it did with our daughter's delivery. The doctor and the midwife pushed and pulled to get the baby out. As soon as I saw him, I shouted, "It's a boy!"

Instead of handing him immediately to my wife to hold him as they had done with our daughter, they whisked him over to the workstation. Jefferson was crying, like a baby should, so we were confused as to why they were starting to wipe him down and suction him out before letting us hold him.

"He's not pinking up," one of the nurses told me as I went over to see my son. Through the army of nurses, I could see he appeared to be breathing but his color was not normal. He was a light blue, grayish color. He looked more like the color of shark than a human. This was not normal. This was not good. They called in a respiratory team.

I tried to push my way closer. I asked hundreds of questions all at once. The nurses blocked my way and ignored me. I became furious and frantic. What was happening to my son?! Why did he look like death?!

The respiratory team arrived and began examining him and I was pushed further out of the way. "There's nothing we can do for him," one of the doctors said.

The Earth stopped moving. Time evaporated. My son, who I had waited to meet for 9 long months, was going to leave me before I even got the chance to touch him. I went empty inside.

As the respiratory team left, the nurses continued to work on him. One of them got on the phone and talked to someone. The rest appeared to be preparing to move him. "Why won't they let me hold him?" I screamed in my head.

Sensing my anxiety and realizing I was about to knock them all down like they were tackling dummies, one of the nurses turned to me and explained that Jefferson was breathing so the reason he wasn't pink had nothing to do with his respiratory system. They believed it was his circulatory system and were prepping him to be moved to a cardiac specialist.

He had my heart already. I wanted to reach into my chest and give mine to him. I wanted him to turn pink, to live, to grow, to become a man. But I couldn't do anything. I couldn't be his father and protect him and hold him and make him better. All I could do was watch as his tiny body writhed and wiggled while cold hands hooked him up to all kinds of devices.

Then, behind me, I noticed something else going on. The doctor and one of the nurses had been sewing up my wife after the C-section and now I heard louder, concerned voices coming from them. I turned around to see them frantically working on my wife.

No. This was not happening.

I turned and grabbed one of the nurses by the arm. "What..." I couldn't say more. My eyes were certainly wild and I knew they were filled because everything was blurry.

"We are having trouble stopping her bleeding," the nurse told me.

Little did I know this was only the beginning of this nightmare.

My son was blue. My wife was bleeding from somewhere. What was I supposed to do? Do I stay with my wife or go with my son? They both needed me.

I acted more than made a decision. As the nurses rushed my son to the NICU, I pulled my hand away from my wife hoping, praying, it would not be the last time I saw her alive, and ran after my son.

When we arrived at the NICU, I managed to get my first close look at my son. His long little fingers wiggled and searched for something to grasp. Instinctively, I stuck my finger out and he grabbed ahold and didn't let go. Everything was blurry again.

The NICU team immediately began tests on Jefferson and discovered he had a congenital heart defect. In his case, they found that his arteries were switched.

He needed heart surgery. Immediately.

They prepped Jefferson for an ambulance ride across town to Children's Mercy hospital where a pediatric cardiologist would essentially keep a small hole in his heart open to temporarily allow his heart to work properly with the help of machines.

The nurses wheeled him to where my wife, thankfully, seemed to be okay from the C-section. She got to see him for the first time. She couldn't hold him. She barely got to touch him. She was able to put her arm through an opening in this plastic box, touch him and talk to him for only a few minutes. I was sad, angry, frustrated but, most of all, deflated.

I was not allowed in the ambulance, something I fought hard to do but lost. The nurses told me to wait 20 minutes before I drove to the hospital so they would have time to get Jefferson ready for his first surgery. I spent the time holding my wife and telling her I would do everything I could to make sure Jefferson came back to her. Alive.

Since I had never been to Children's Mercy, I fumbled my way there, making several wrong turns and probably going way over the speed limit. I parked. Somewhere. And probably illegally. I rushed through the emergency room doors and was greeted by one of the nurses who said frustrated, "We've been waiting for you."

Apparently there were papers to sign before Jefferson could go into surgery and either they forgot to tell me or did not believe I would really wait the 20 minutes. All I thought, though, was I had failed as his father. Minutes were precious. I wasted a few of them that could have meant the difference between his life and death.

I placed both my hands on his box, got as close to him as possible and told him I loved him and would be right here when he got out of surgery. The nurses took him into the operating room and I was directed to the waiting room.

The doctors and nurses were vague with all their information. This really pissed me off. I like to know what is going on. I like to be in control. But I knew almost nothing. I didn't know how serious this surgery was or how long it might take. I didn't know this was only the first of several surgeries he would have to have assuming he made it through this one.

Not knowing how long I would be waiting and realizing my cell phone didn't work in the waiting room, I went down the hall to where my cell phone would work and called my wife.

She didn't answer. Her sister did.

"Where's Kristine?" I asked.

"She's in the ER getting a CT scan," my sister-in-law told me.

My wife's twin sister is an athletic trainer and understands a lot about the human body. I knew she would tell me how serious it is.

"The doctors think she might be bleeding internally," she told me. Then, much softer, she hauntingly said, "It's not good, Joseph."

This is not happening, I thought. This can't be happening!

I clicked 'End' on my phone and started walking back to the operating room. I happened to notice the time on phone and my heart dropped to the floor. WHERE IS MY DAUGHTER?!

By this time, our family should have been together in our antepartum room at the hospital. My wife was there while Jefferson and I were across town in another hospital and I didn't even know where my daughter was or who was taking care of her. At that moment, with my wife in ER, my son in surgery and my daughter God knows where, I believed I had lost my entire family. They were all gone.

I glanced out the window of the waiting room. Outside, cars and buses were whizzing by. People were busily shopping or taking a mid-day run. The grass was the greenest it had been yet that spring. The sun was bright. The sky was clear and blue like the ocean.

Everywhere the world was going on with its regular business on one of the most beautiful and peaceful days of the year. Inside that waiting room, my world had stopped. I was alone. I began to cry. And cry. And cry.

I prayed to God. I blamed God. I waited.

After about three hours, which felt like 300 years, the doctor came into the waiting room. Jefferson had made it through the surgery like a champ. They ballooned his heart to keep a small hole opened in it so it would keep beating. They would do a follow-up surgery to switch the arteries as soon as he was strong enough.

I thanked the doctor and rushed out of the waiting room to a place where my cell phone would work so I could find out about my wife. She answered the phone and it was the most beautiful sound I heard that day. She, too, was ok. The CT scan showed she wasn't bleeding internally. I then called my wife's parents, who were still watching our daughter, to explain what had happened.

When I first saw Jefferson after surgery, a giant lump entered my throat that didn't leave for weeks. This tiny, thankfully now pink, baby had so many wires attached to him; he looked like he was in the middle of a plate of colored spaghetti.

It was two days before the nurses would let me hold him. When I did, I didn't let go of him for 12 hours. All the tests, feedings, and diaper changes were done with me holding him.

When I wasn't holding him, I was always near him, always talking to him. The nurses finally started making up excuses to get me to leave so I could take a shower or get something to eat or go to the bathroom. I didn't care about me but they knew I needed to take care of myself for Jefferson.

On the fourth day of Jefferson's life, my wife was released from the hospital and brought to Children's Mercy. She wasn't allowed to walk, but she was there. I handed Jefferson to her so she could hold him for the first time in his life. It's what I needed to know it was going to be okay. Everything was going to be okay. It was one of the better moments in my life.

We were prepared for Jefferson to have his second surgery to switch his arteries when he was eighteen days old. We sat in the waiting room with our family members around us, waiting for the regular updates from the operating room. They called us to a private room for the first update and the doctor came in. He said they were stopping the surgery. I didn't know what to say or how to react. They thought he had an infection and wanted to make sure before doing the surgery.

They sent us back to the ICU and for ten agonizing days, we waited for the doctors to give the clearance for him to go back on the operating table. At 28 days old, Jefferson went back into surgery. He made it through with flying colors and only seven days later, we were on our way home.

We learned later that of all the congenital heart defects, this was the best one to have since surgeons have been performing this surgery for over 25 years. After his arterial repair surgery, he has no restrictions and should not need any additional surgeries.

To see him today, you would never know he went through this traumatic ordeal. He is like every other toddler: rambunctious, full of energy and throws a fair number of tantrums.

I feel so fortunate my family remained intact but the experience still haunts me. I was so helpless while so much has happening to my family.

Sometimes when I look at my son, all I see are the needles and wires that were once attached to his tiny, fragile body.

And I cry.

PART TWO

BREAKING THE MOLD

"It made financial sense for me to be the one at home and neither of us had a preconceived notion that genitalia are what determine your ability to raise a kid or operate a vacuum cleaner."

- Chad Welch, father of 2 boys from St. Peters, MO

TEARS OF OUR FATHERS

Eric Jefferson, Chicago, IL

I'm watching a slide show of other men's families flash across the overhead projection screen in a fluorescent-lit classroom at the 18th Annual At-Home Dads Convention in Denver, Colorado. A moment ago, I was eating a cupcake topped with bacon… because that's how (some) men do it. I watch with detached interest as little faces, little hands, big eyes, and gigantic dreamers click across the screen.

After a few minutes though, the room grows silent; disturbed only by laughter at behind-the-scenes antics each of us can imagine by looking at this one frame. Each picture is just one sliver of a moment and I, like most in the room, don't know more than a handful of the children in the video. Some are alone with hilarious expressions. Others are with their siblings playing or holding hands. There are more still with mom or dad embracing or sharing silly costumes with their children.

Now droplets spilling over the dam of my eyelids have caught me by surprise. What trickery is this!? Why the water works? This is a man's convention, a dad's convention dammit! Aren't we supposed to be too hungover to make it to the presentations? Shouldn't we be considering cutting out early to check out a strip club? What is going on here?!

When it comes to fathers who don't follow society's rules, I suppose I shouldn't be surprised to find that what might look like a glorified guy's weekend away to the casual observer turns out to be so much more. I look to my right: red eyes. I look to my left and that dude has a tissue at his face. Everyone looks as stunned as I am to have been caught off guard by family pictures, but no one is ashamed. We share these feelings. We let them roll over us. We are the same.

We've talked about communicating effectively, about being engaged. We've heard stories of loss and triumph. We've listened to raconteurs deliver heart-wrenching descriptions of miracles. We've laughed at each other's anecdotes about the challenges of being an at-home parent. We've heard quotes such as: "Potty training isn't a corridor, it's a labyrinth" (Chris Routly of www.DaddyDoctrines.com). We've learned breathing exercises from Dr. Rich Mahogany of ManTherapy.org. We all wanted to hug National At-Home Dad Network President Al Watts as he painted a picture for us, with a croaking voice, of his 11-year old daughter falling off a horse into a canyon and surviving. The pain he felt, the feelings of helplessness he endured as he waited for her to be extracted via helicopter, pierced us all like a dagger. The sheer force of will he showed to get through the epic story for us became our strength and we helped feed it within him.

The weekend was an incredible experience. I've met dozens of guys for the first time and others I only knew from social media. I've ribbed and joked with men as if we were old buddies, then turned around and had conversations with them I'd be surprised to have with my closest friends. There were beers, bourbon and burgers with guys who will make your stomach hurt from laughter. I've listened to stories of sorrow, tragedy, intestinal fortitude, persistence and honor in the face of challenges. Sure, many of us partied and carried on, but we were careful to pull back the reins so as not to miss out on an opportunity to learn and share with these fathers.

As I sit here watching the faces of children I've never met go by on the screen, those faces stop being strangers and they start to represent fatherhood in general for me. They show how much we have in common despite our differences, and they are the thread that hold all in attendance together. We're lashed together by the common purpose of raising great children and becoming the best fathers we can be.

Somehow the grins going by cease to be just some kids and they start to look like loved members of my community. I see determination in their eyes. I see wonder, love, and innocence in every smile. I see faces looking for approval they readily receive from loving parents. I'm reminded of the stories I've heard this week and suddenly all of the stories I've heard of pain and encouragement of miracles and disasters have become my own. I'm crying with joy for these families and my own.

These dads demonstrated how we should define masculinity; with strength and support for each other and for our families, with empathy and encouragement for all in our community and many beyond, through teaching and in listening we teach our boys and girls what a man is… what a dad is.

A MUCH NEEDED DIVORCE

Matt Peregoy, Finksburg, MD

Sometimes, a divorce is necessary in order for you to become the father you know you want to be. Sometimes, a divorce is the only way you can fully rid yourself of excuses for why you are not the father you know you can be. Sometimes, a divorce inspires you to become the husband you know you should be. And sometimes, you may have to divorce yourself from something that is consuming your life in order to fully embrace the family you should have been embracing all along. Here is my divorce story.

I walked in the door with a Ricky-like, "Honey, I'm home!" fully expecting the residents of my kingdom (my wife and daughter) to be excited for me to be home at a decent hour. My expectations came crashing down when I walked into the living room. My wife was sitting on the floor, in tears, holding our crying daughter. "I can't do this alone anymore," she sobbed. Those words cut me deep, like a spoon in the heart, dull and painful beyond all explanation.

I was blissfully unaware of the stress my wife was experiencing while raising our baby girl. She was essentially a single mother for an entire year while I was working between sixty and seventy hours a week at my job as a newly promoted retail store manager. I would often leave the house before she woke, and sneak back in long after dinner was cold, sometimes after she was asleep. I was always on call, and always working late. I worked every weekend and holiday for a salary with no overtime. I felt like I was married to my job and parenting my employees. While I was pursuing success via sales and profit bonuses, my wife was keeping the house, walking the dog, shoveling the snow, pumping the milk, doing the doctor visits, not to mention caring for every other need of our breastfeeding infant.

In that moment, my wife made a desperate plea for me to be more present in our home. We began a series of conversations that lead to me becoming an at-home dad. I had believed I was doing my part by bringing home a paycheck, but there was so much more! I needed to be participating in raising our child and pulling my weight around the house as well. I needed to be a better husband and father, and my job was my excuse for not accomplishing it.

So, I divorced my job. I let my employees be adopted by the succeeding manager. They're all doing just fine. I do miss them sometimes, but my new job as an at-home father is the most rewarding career I have ever pursued. I get to see the fruit of my labor every day as I watch my child grow. I can invest my quality time into her development and well-being. My quality of life has improved, my parenting skills have improved and, most importantly, my marriage has improved as a result of me getting honest with myself about my addiction to work. By being totally open with my spouse, I was able to make the changes I needed to give my family a better life.

You might not want to be a stay-at-home dad like me, but there may be a dozen other ways you can improve the quality of life for your family. Ask yourself if you are addicted to anything that keeps you away from them. Be honest about your excuses for not being the husband or father you want to be. Man up and take the positive steps to fix those areas. Maybe, like me, a divorce from those excuses is in order. I promise the happiness your family will experience as a result of the divorce from your excuses will outweigh any pain you experience by divorcing them.

FAMILY IS FIRST

Chris Middleton, Oviedo, FL

In 2001, our first son, Joshua, was born two days after 9/11. It was a happy ending to an otherwise miserable week. He had been born several weeks early so we anticipated there might be some delays in his development. As he approached his second birthday, it was clear he was going to need physical, speech and language therapy. My wife and I decided to exercise our liberal (two year) leave policy at work and I became an at-home dad so one of us could be more available.

Little did I know, as a new dad, how much I would gain from spending time with my son. He helped me realize how much of an impact we as dads can have on our children and the security that comes from having someone at home nurturing them versus a paid caregiver.

Taking two years away from my career, we knew, would have an impact on my advancement opportunities but our priorities had changed. Our focus became "family first." As my two-year leave was ending, our second son was born. My wife decided to take her two-year leave and stay at home while I went back to work.

In 2006, my wife returned to work as the economy began to falter. Downsizing became the norm around the country. The company I worked for went through a restructuring but, instead of getting laid off, I was offered a different job. My wife and I decided to decline it. We chose to live off her income and have me stay home so we could maintain a strong, stable, and more predictable upbringing for our boys. Staying home has given me the opportunity to invest in our sons' lives while being a role model to other dads who struggle with balancing work and family.

Allowing me to stay home with our two boys has been one of the best gifts a wife could ever give her husband. There have certainly been many challenges but the benefits to our family far outweigh them.

In 2008, as an active parent member of the local PTA, I began to have a vision of rallying dads at the school to get involved in their children's education beyond helping with homework. I explored the national initiatives already in place and settled on exploring one from nearby Tampa, FL called All Pro Dads, associated with Family First, a non-profit organization that helps strengthen families. Tony Dungy, former head coach of the Tampa Bay Buccaneers and Indianapolis Colts, was a co-founder of this initiative back in 1997 and I've always been a big fan of his, so that didn't hurt either.

I decided to start a chapter at my son's elementary school. We held our first event (Donuts with Dad) and had a line of dads waiting to get in to sit with their child and chat about life. About 450 dads showed up, representing 60% of the school's fathers. It was a success beyond my wildest predictions!

Clearly, there was a need and interest from dads to get involved with their children's lives at school. Since then, we've continued to build on this theme and added speakers at a breakfast event, outings to sporting events and even a Bike Rodeo run by the dads. To get even more involved with my son's school, I've done some substitute teaching, not so much for the paycheck, but so I can keep an ear to the curriculum being taught and stay in tune with what challenges are ahead for our boys. It has also helped me gain a better appreciation for our kids' teachers and what they are up against in educating our next generation.

I am very grateful for being in a position where I can make a lasting impact on society and, most importantly, my family. The sacrifices we made as a family will undoubtedly pay dividends for years to come. So, in this way, not having a "traditional job" has helped me focus more attention on my most important job: fatherhood.

I DON'T BABYSIT

Jameson Mercier, Plantation, FL

For the last few years now, I have been home with my kids off and on. My job is such that I do not have to be at the office everyday; nor do I need to stay all day when I do go in. This has allowed me to spend more time at home with my family and be more actively engaged with my children.

I am grateful for this opportunity to spend so much time with my kids. However, there is another aspect for which I am also very appreciative. In being home with my kids, I have learned a lot about society and their views on parenting; particularly dads and parenting.

While I am not an at-home-dad exclusively, on average, I am home two or three days a week. On the days when I am home, I sometimes engage in a ritual performed by much of our species. This is a ritual I have observed first-hand. I have studied it and have become quite competent in the performance of this ritual. It only occurs at predetermined locations, but there is no set time.

This ritual of gathering food and supplies is widely known as "grocery shopping". It requires a lot of preparation and can be a major undertaking for the inexperienced. I round up my young and load them in the minivan (similar to a car, except with more room for diapers, strollers, bags, toys, etc). Once everyone is loaded and accounted for, we head off.

Since I began taking my kids with me, I noticed I have become somewhat of an attraction. While collecting navel oranges and checking for the perfect apples and bananas, I notice stares and hear things like "Ooo" and "Oh my." On occasion, some observers have even been brave enough to cautiously approach my bunch and me and ask questions.

On one occasion, I had this exchange with a lady:

"So mom needed a break, huh?"

"Excuse me?" I replied.

"That's nice," she said as she walked away.

This is pretty much how it goes when we wander beyond the confines of our domicile. The conversations and comments are pretty much identical. It doesn't matter if we're at Target, CVS, Costco, or the library.

One morning, I was once again engaged in my ritual of gathering food when a gentleman began to circle us. I first thought this was strange, but then I thought perhaps he wanted to get to the strawberries we were collecting. I looked up again to see him standing there just watching us. After a moment, he smiled and asked, "So you're babysitting?"

"Excuse me?" I replied.

"That's good. Good for you," he said as he walked away.

As a father of three, it is my responsibility and pleasure to care for my children and spend time with them. Truth be told, there are days I enjoy their company more than some adults I know.

I find the notion that men who are home with their children are "babysitting" to be beyond ridiculous, not to mention ignorant. Since when were fathers expected to babysit rather than care for their own children? Furthermore, society says they want fathers to be present and involved. Yet when they are, these men are regarded as strange. Why is it that people turn their heads and point when they see a father pushing a stroller or changing a diaper?

The challenges of being a parent are tough enough without having to deal with other people's issues and ill-informed expectations. So next time you see us in our family wagon or in Publix picking blueberries, don't stand off in the distance staring and taking pictures. The flash hurts our eyes.

In case you missed it, I don't babysit. I am a father.

WHO YOU CALLIN' MR. MOM?

Jeffrey Davis, Canyon, TX

In the days leading up to the birth of my son, I tried to prepare myself for all the changes that would be coming. I had some idea of what it might be like to deal with midnight feedings, constant diaper changes and an end to what little social life I had. I steeled myself to the potential of postpartum depression, wifely hormonal changes and a drastically altered sex life. And, of course, I attended to the usual daddy details like getting the little guy's crib, changing station and clothing storage ready. While I tried not to become convinced I knew it all (and boy, did I NOT know it all), I felt about as prepared as I was going to be for the wave of change about to crash into my life.

There was one change I never saw coming, though. I'm not a member of the He-man Woman Hater's Club. I'm not a "bro", and I don't pride myself on being manlier than the next guy. But I do like classic cars. I like to hunt, even if it just ends up being an armed hike. I have a very respectable collection of tools hanging on the wall of my garage and I spend a lot of weekends turning a wrench. I would definitely rather watch *Robocop* or a *Rocky* marathon than the latest chick-flick. I even sport a beard no lady outside of a sideshow could compete with. I don't think there's much chance of anyone confusing me with a woman. So imagine my shock when friends, family members, neighbors and even chance acquaintances on the street called me "Mr. Mom."

It started with the principal of the school where I taught. When I told her I would not be returning the next school year in order to work at night and take care of my son during the day, she gifted me with the moniker for the first time. The superintendent of schools reinforced it by tossing it off in the middle of a meeting a couple of weeks later. Over the next few months, as we continued to prepare for the summer arrival of my son, I would hear it over and over again. I can accept the fact that my son is several orders of magnitude cuter than I am and that people only get excited to see me coming when I have him in my arms. I am okay with being merely a transportation system for the little lump of adorability I helped create. But this child has a mother, and I am not okay with being called "Mr. Mom."

Strangely, the most common place to hear the word was from the very people who should have known better: women, who have been on the short end of the sexism stick for most of human history. Women, who would have been immensely offended if anyone dared to call them "Mrs. Dad" when they headed off to work. Maybe these women felt the same way seeing a man caring for his child during normal business hours as men did seeing their wives riveting steel girders and building Buicks when they returned from World War II. Threatened, in other words, with their place in our society.

My mantra is not a call to arms for dads, whether working or staying at home. I am not trying to start or even continue a fight with the women in our lives. Believe me, there are plenty of sleepless nights and teething-fueled cry-fests for all the sexes to have a hand in raising our kids. We would only be doing ourselves a disservice by doing anything to drive a wedge between the mothers of our children and us. Instead, this is about reassuring what you are doing as a stay-at-home-dad does not make you any less of a man. This is a reminder that taking care of kids all day is one of the most mentally and physically exhausting jobs there is, and your buddy who spent eight hours at his cushy office job and then got to sleep all night has got nothing on you. This is a reminder that you, my brother fathers, do not have to sit there and take the name calling and the derision from people who see you out there doing the things they wish their fathers had done with them. Instead, you can respond like a gentleman and remind those who would sneer and make snide remarks about what you do that we already have a title. We are Dad, and we are fiercely proud of it.

LOVING MY RED-HEADED STEP-CHILD

Jeff Hay, Kelowna, British Columbia

I have had the opportunity to work with other people's children and treat them as my own through various jobs running a childcare center, directing a summer camp, and years spent teaching and coaching. However, now I am treating and loving another man's son as my own. It is a wonderful and challenging opportunity.

Years ago, I heard a comedian make the comment, *"I am going to work you like a red-headed step child."* This made me both laugh and cringe; now I have a red-headed step son!

Four minutes into my blind date with his mother, we discovered we both had young boys named William. Our attraction was strong, so this was not a deal breaker.

As our relationship grew, we introduced my son and daughter to her son and as the months passed, we let them decide what to call each other. At first, it was step brother and step sister, but happily it has just morphed into brother and sister. Now almost three years in, it is hilarious to hear my daughter introduce her brothers to strangers, *"This is my brother Will and my other brother Will!"*

At least it isn't "Daryl."

Given our past failed marriages, neither of us was in a hurry to get married. We were just enjoying our second chance at happiness and raising our 'step' children together.

We have tried everything to differentiate the boys "Big/Little Will, Bill, Willie." Nothing worked until a friend jokingly suggested using their ages. So now we have Will 8 and Will 6 (or 'Eighter' and 'Sixer').

If someone asks, I say I have three children. And I do. I feel and know it. But it is different. For two of my children, I have been there since the first tummy kicks and I helped deliver them both into this world. For my red-headed step-son, I didn't meet him until he was four.

Blending a family effectively requires a slow pace and much thought to the implications for the kids. Early on, I was in awe of how easily my partner welcomed my children into her heart. I honestly believe she loves my children as much as her own natural son.

Do women just have a greater capacity in their hearts to love? Or is it because she had a much more open and inclusive sense that families come in all shapes and sizes, while I was still grieving the loss of my family unit and the "white picket fence" dream?

I have lots of love to give, but early on, it didn't flow as naturally from me to her son. If I am being truly honest, when I was watching the kids play, my eyes would naturally find my son and daughter, while I would actively have to think to watch Will 6.

I found this both mysterious and very troubling. It wasn't that I didn't love and care for her son, but it just wasn't the same. I would see him differently; his actions and behavior would register differently.

Will 6 has a living, present, active, and loving dad. I am not replacing an absent or deceased dad. Will 6 has a great relationship with his dad and I know nothing I do will take away from their solid relationship.

As a step-dad, I need to honor his dad and carve out my own relationship with Will 6. I want to be much more than just a "cool uncle" type. I want him to look to me for guidance, comfort, and discipline. While he still defers to his mom when knees are skinned and for late night frights, he knows I am also there and a pretty solid second choice. He has the wonderful gift of two dads – his real dad and his "bald daddy!"

Canadian parenting icon Gordon Neufeld declared, "The only true authority we have with our children is the authority they are willing to grant us through their desire to maintain a strong relationship with us." I think this is even truer when raising step-children.

I have to earn Will 6's respect. I cannot demand it; that will only lead to more problems. I must take a more roundabout way into his heart. Without the luxury of years spent together, I try to maximize our time together to continue strengthening our bond.

During my difficult divorce, I felt, at times, my bond with my own children being strained and threatened. Looking back, I know I focused too much attention on them out of guilt for what they had been through, at the cost of building my new relationship with Will 6.

Had I been more secure and confident in my bonds with my own children, perhaps Will 6 and I could be further down the path together. But we are finding our way together quickly, creating our own fun memories and rituals *("Wake up time with Dr. Crush!")*.

In the early blending days, there were definitely silent battles between the children to be next to me for movies or books at bedtime. There was also a lot of acceptance, resilience and understanding from all three of the children as they had all been through the same thing.

Now my children are just fine with sharing their dad. I do try to spend equal individual time with all three so they each feel special and unique. I always strive for equality.

As Will 6's step-dad, it is critically important to me that he feels and knows he is equally important to me and is not at the bottom of my hierarchy. I love my one-on-one time with him and whether we are off to a hockey game or the video game arcade, I feel new bonds of love growing all the time.

There are definitely growing pains as a family is blended together. I hate admitting I favored my children early on, in terms of who got the benefit of the doubt when battles and situations happened. Nowadays, if I am still being honest, I probably favor Will 6 more!

The ultimate goal is to be a positive force in all my children's lives. I want to be a strong male role model: the beacon to look to – for guidance, morality, ethics, and love.

While I wish it was totally natural and organic for me, the family assimilation came much more quickly and easily for my partner. One thing is for certain, the children are even better at it than both of us.

TWO MOMS?

Shawn LaTourette, Highland Park, NJ

Recently, an aunt told me our now seventeen month-old twins were "so lucky" because "it's like they have two moms." I smiled a self-congratulatory smile and thanked her for what she meant as a compliment. Days later, my mind returned to her comment. It was odd, I thought, almost offensive. To be sure, I am quite pleased the hours of thankless work I pour into caring for this rather high-maintenance pair do not go unnoticed. Still, I was left thinking about whether my fathering was so laudable. Let's say I am a veritable rock star dad. If my parenting rises to such heights, must it be deemed motherly? And if so, what does it say about our perceptions and expectations of fatherhood (or manhood for that matter) when we characterize a father as less capable of, or more deserving of, praise for simple acts of parenting? Are not all parents created equal?

Tradition may paint women as nurturers and men as providers. I have never thought of these roles as mutually exclusive, and my wife and I do our best to parent as equally as we can. We play to our strengths, and there are certainly elements of parenting at which one or the other of us excels, while the other flounders. Although my wife may spend more overall time parenting than me, I am no mere babysitter. In fact, I feel just as capable at my night job where I try to use my improvised lullabies to convince wound-up toddlers to settle down and sleep, as I do at my day job where I try to convince judges my clients are on the right side of the law. Still, I get the sense that society does not expect me, as a man, to feel so deeply connected to my children, let alone become confident, capable and involved in their care.

I got this message loud and clear as a newly minted lawyer grinding the gears of the corporate legal machine. "BigLaw," as they call it, takes great pride in its female lawyers—as well it should—and seeks to accommodate them within, what is often, a rigid profession. BigLaw boasts its flexible, work-life balanced schedule of reduced billable hours for those who have family obligations. With such programs designed to retain female lawyers, BigLaw has become friendlier to mothers, but not to all parents alike. It remains a boys club, where the men are lawyers first. When my twins arrived, I knew I could not be a father first and remain in BigLaw's good graces. I toyed with the idea of being the first man in my firm to demand the work-life balance schedule, but my superiors freely admitted doing so would signal the beginning of the end of my BigLaw career. So, I left BigLaw and kept my parental dignity.

Today, I wake with my early-rising twins, take them on a morning run and cook them breakfast, before heading to my second job. I sing them to sleep most weeknights, and on weekends I tend to take responsibility for steering the twinsanity express while my wife enjoys the view from the backseat. It is hard work to be sure, and it should be recognized. Not because I am a man doing the exceptional, but because I am a parent raising children. So, the next time I roll the twins into a coffee shop after our Saturday morning stroll and someone half-asks, "So, you're on duty today," I should be honest. I'm on duty EVERY DAY. And, if ever I get another comment about how lucky my twins are to have two mothers, I will stand up for fatherhood; for my belief that fathers should act and be treated like full parents.

When I next see that aunt, I will have to tell her my fatherly motivation is rather simple: I want my children to grow up knowing that either of their parents can readily meet their needs. I may not have breastfed my twins, and I certainly could not have birthed them (their mom got me there!). But, I can certainly feed and groom them, help them make a joyfully tremendous mess (and then clean it up), wake with them in the middle of the night, comfort them when they're sad, soothe them when they're sick (and get sick all over me), encourage them to wear a jacket, to work hard even when it's not fun, to be brave when they're scared, and to find what moves them the way they move me. This is what every parent does.

I have realized I am not my twins' second mom.

I am their dad.

DADDYING WITH DOCTORS

Sean Rose, Lewisburg, TN

"Sickle Cell Disease is color blind." This became my motto as I embraced the birth of our third daughter and, with it, a diagnosis that was not only foreign to us, but carried a lifetime of complications, restrictions and stereotypes.

When the doctor revealed Sophia's diagnosis, I was not only devastated but also deeply puzzled.

What is Sickle Cell Disease?

How did my daughter get it?

Why Sophia?

Is she going to die?

My mind raced a thousand miles a minute as I tried fervently to wrap my head around the doctor's words. Sophia looked so healthy. My darling baby couldn't possibly have this "disease". Nevertheless, I embraced her and the unknown territory and challenges that lay ahead.

I scoured the Internet, gleaning medical journals, blogs and Facebook to connect with other families of children with Sickle Cell Disease in search of any information to help me better understand the disease. I was desperate to educate myself by any means possible so my wife and I could give the care our angel needed.

One of the first things I learned was that Sickle Cell Disease is very rare for Caucasians. In the United States, nearly all cases are of African or Hispanic descent. My baby, my little Irish princess, was embarking on uncharted territory.

In addition to the race myth about Sickle Cell Disease, I also dealt with the unfortunate stigma of fathers as primary caregivers. Our society commonly believes dads are not able to nurture or care for children to the same capacity as a mom. Often, nurses and doctors were condescending, asking why my wife wasn't there or, worse, not willing to treat our daughter until they talked to my wife. The acceptance of Sickle Cell Disease as a possibility and my role as her primary caregiver would create challenges I could not have foreseen and would change me in ways I never thought possible.

I was what my family and friends considered quiet, laid-back, even too calm at times. But my daughter needed a fighter - someone to step up to the plate and duke it out to make sure she was getting the best care. As her dad, her primary caregiver, I had to find my voice regardless of what others said. I had to be what she needed. I had to be more than I was.

Sophia's chronic illness causes excruciating pain. She will curl up in a ball and go into a pain-induced "sleep" until we can convince the doctors to administer narcotics. During one particularly severe episode, I sat with Sophia in the emergency room waiting for what seemed like an eternity. When the doctor finally entered, she took one glance at Sophia and promptly said, "You're white, you can't have Sickle Cell! Why would you waste our time bringing your daughter in here for a simple headache?" She turned around to leave.

Aghast at her blatant bias and unprofessional bedside manner, I moved in front of the door, blocking her from leaving. "I am not only her father, but ALSO her primary caretaker," I began, my temper uncharacteristically rising. "I was there the day she was diagnosed, the day she had heart surgery and the day she had her first blood transfusion. My daughter is in PAIN and you WILL take care of her the same way you would if her mother had brought her."

The speechless doctor immediately typed in the orders for prescription pain meds and then silently left the exam room. From then on, I found myself transforming into a verbally assertive, action-oriented advocate. My friends and family even started calling me Sophia's personal social worker.

As the years rolled by, my role as Sophia's day-to-day caregiver became more deeply seeded within the minds of the doctors. Routine visits, late nights in the emergency room and long stays on the inpatient wing finally persuaded the staff I was not just a "stand-in" for her mother. The medical staff within the Pediatric Sickle Cell Clinic began to place value on my opinion. I was commissioned to sit on the Governor's Advisory Board for Sickle Cell Disease, a position I continue to hold to this day. In addition, I assist medical professionals on providing better parental instructions regarding this complicated disease. My opinion has value. My voice carries weight. My willingness and determination to break through the barriers regarding fatherhood have allowed me to not only level the playing field for dads, but has also opened the eyes of the medical staff to the importance of fathers.

One night, as we waited for a resource nurse to draw Sophia's blood, my sickly two-year-old turned slowly toward me and whispered, "Tank you dada." Tears streamed down my cheek as I kissed her hand and held her close. Her "thank you" is all I need to keep fighting all day, every day, for her and the other forgotten children that Sickle Cell Disease has enveloped.

To learn more about what you can do for children affected with Sickle Cell Disease, please visit www.HopeforSCD.org.

UNLEASHING A FATHER'S LOVE

Don Jackson, Albuquerque, NM

I love my son! I love to express my love for him whenever I can with a hug and lots of kisses, even in public. I also enjoy snuggling with him. When I do, I sometimes feel the uncomfortable stares of strangers.

At first, I thought it might be me. Perhaps it was my imagination or paranoia. However, I've discovered I'm not the only dad who has hugged his child and felt the judgement of others.

I network with a group of Dad Bloggers. Like me, these fellow dads enjoy expressing love to their children in public. These dads have also experienced the trepidation of other people when they share tender moments of intimacy with their children. My fellow loving, involved dads and I are confused by the reaction we receive and don't understand the mindset. We are expressing our love for our children. What can be wrong with that?

Many moms and parenting experts proclaim that men, especially dads, need to show more love and affection toward their children. Yet, our culture struggles to accept and embrace dads who express and share intimate moments with their children.

In some ways, I understand the skepticism and suspicious glances men receive when they are around children. I know there are people who mistreat and do unspeakable things to children. Most of those people are men. However, Dr. Gene Abel, the leading researcher in studies of sexual behavior problems in the U.S., estimates that only between 1% and 5% of our population molest children[14]. Child sex abuse is a real problem parents must protect their children from but, fortunately, it is rare.

Still, I must admit I have been guilty of distrusting my fellow man. When a woman approaches my son with a smile and points out his cuteness, I'm

---

[14] Rowland, Rhonda (October 16, 1994). Thieves of Childhood, *CNN*

comfortable with her behavior. If a man, however, approaches my son in a similar manner, I experience immediate anxiety. I'm doing my best to change the way I react to other men because if I would like to see change, it must begin with me.

I agree we should protect our children from sexual predators. I know we all want to protect our children from every evil in this world, but do we have to look at everything around us (second guessing everyone and everything), seeing everyone as a potential threat to our children?

Do we need to be that callous - that jaded?

Have we, as a society, forgotten the truth that "it takes a village"?

Why should we look at men in a funny way when they are affectionate with their children?

Isn't this the level of intimacy we want from dads?

There is darkness in our world and people who mean to do harm to our children. If we fail to see beyond the murky darkness in the hearts of the few of those who would do our children wrong, we miss out on the intimate moments our children could experience with the rest of the wonderful people who really love and care about the safety of our children.

The truth is, good and well-behaved dads far out number irresponsible dads who place children in harms way or mistreat them. I feel it is time to re-evaluate our thought processes. There are men who truly love their children, love to cuddle, kiss and hug their children. They should be celebrated, not judged as potential predators.

Today's dads are taking care of their families, building healthy and loving relationships with their kids, and doing their best to be great fathers. When a man approaches our children we shouldn't make a judgment call on whether he is a threat or not. Instead we should respond to him the same way we do a woman: embrace his kindness and use it as an opportunity to get to know him better.

I realize there may come a day when my son won't like me to kiss and hug him in public. Nevertheless, I will continue to show my love as often as possible. I hope my actions will help him develop a greater level of comfort and confidence to publicly express his love for his children when he becomes a dad than I have had as his dad.

WHILE YOU LIVE, SHINE

Chris Bernholdt, Devon, PA

I feel like Rodney Dangerfield. Sometimes, I just don't get any respect. Such is the life of a stay-at-home dad. We have to learn how to shine. I have met plenty of moms who think that me staying at home is such a great thing. Because let's face it, it shouldn't matter what my gender is; the job is the same. Maybe the way I approach it is different but I still bandage boo-boos, make lunches and clean up puke.

There are some moms, though, who don't get it.

My daughter had been talking about this friend of hers in kindergarten for some time, so I contacted her mom through the class email list to try to set up a play date for her and her new friend. After much back and forth about where, when, what time etc., we made the play date and I brought my daughter to her new friend's house.

Before I left, the mom and I asked her about what she did, what her husband did, and how long they had lived in the area. I got to know her a little before I left my child with her and soon she redirected some questions back at me.

"Soooo, what do you do?" she asked.

"I am a stay-at-home dad," I said confidently.

She laughed.

Yes. Laughed. I felt a little ashamed though I never had before. People act surprised or shocked to find out I stay home with our kids, but I have never been laughed at.

I tried to let it roll off my back and kept talking, adding that I was a blogger... more laughter. Then I quickly added, "I am a part of the National At-Home Dad Network and we have a convention every year." More laughter.

"Are you serious?" she asked through her you-have-got-to-be-kidding-me grin.

"Yes, it has been pretty awesome for me," I replied, reasserting myself. "So much so that I started my own Philly Dads Group. Maybe your husband would be interested?" and I handed over my card.

She stood there, stunned. "That's what my husband wishes he could do," she finally said, her grin melting. "He is stuck with his family business and would rather stay at home. In fact, I wish he would too."

I am not sure if she was trying to save face but she added, "Looks like there is a whole other world that I just don't know about." Sure. That's it. Although you would have to be living under a rock to not hear about how roles of caregivers have changed in the last ten years. Changing people's minds doesn't happen overnight though. Hopefully, I opened up her eyes to how seriously some dads embrace this role for their families.

While it is rare to have this kind of reaction, I have received strange stares at the grocery store in the middle of the day and have heard ignorant comments from strangers I meet that think I am "babysitting my kids for a few hours." Often, I have to remind myself I am doing well for my family, I am not doing it for anyone else. Some people understand. This is not a joke to me; this is my life.

When I returned home, I received an email from my dad telling me about something he learned from a music class called the "Epitaph of Seikilos" taken from the first century. This song represents the earliest record of a full composition and what was inscribed on someone's tombstone between 200 BC and 100 AD. Roughly translated, it means:

"While you live, shine. Let nothing trouble you. Life is only too short, and time takes its toll."

Amazing the way the universe works. When I was feeling challenged by those who might bring me down, my own father lifted me back up. We cannot be mired by the doubters who seek to bring us down. Instead, it is us who must change skewed perceptions back to reality and make others see the light. I know what I am doing with the time I have, and I aim to make a difference in this world. Maybe with help, they will see me shine.

I wouldn't be human if I didn't want people to think highly of me. As a stay-at-home parent there are no accolades; no one is taking you out to a fancy dinner to thank you for your work on a project. There is no pin for years of service.

Stay-at-home dads are looking to blow the doors off the perception that men have to be pigeonholed into traditional roles. I assume men in professions where other males are not "typically" seen, like in nursing, have faced similar struggles. But do we call every male nurse we meet Gaylord Focker? No, but people still refer to stay-at-home dads as "Mr. Mom." It needs to change.

My time with my kids has been my composition in progress. I have, with my wife's help, shaped my kids into the people they will be one note at a time. In every job I have held, I have sought to make a difference in the lives of children. Staying at home is my opus and I hope more people will just give it a listen.

While I live, I will shine.

PART THREE

EARNING THE DAD BADGE

"I remember a time when I thought I had stumped Jerrod, my four-year old son, by asking him what Batman's super power was. He thought about it and then answered, 'Money.' I was floored. Thirty years of idolizing Batman and I'd never thought of it that way but he was absolutely correct."
- *Gerald Plummer, father of one from Burbank, CA*

NIGHT BECOMES US

Ben Petrick, Hillsboro, OR

from *Forty Thousand to One* with Scott Brown
Copyright 2011 KMP Enterprises. Reprinted with permission.

Every parent knows what it's like to wake up in the middle of the night and find your child standing next to the bed saying, "I had a bad dream." Most of us — though not all of us — can do something to soothe them.

When you're among those who can't soothe because you are physically unable, "defeated" doesn't even begin to describe the emotion. The chronically ill all long for "normalcy," and never more than when we want to calm our babies' fears.

My four-year-old daughter's voice woke me up at 2:30 a.m. recently. It was a moment I'd been waiting for since the day she was born.

At night, I don't take any medication for my Parkinson's disease because in the long run, it has a corrosive effect.

Prior to my second DBS surgery, I was basically straddling a fence. I was utterly frozen without my medication; rendered as inert as a statue. On the flipside, taking the medication I required exacerbated its side effects to an ever-increasing degree.

So in the evening, I'd go without medicine, ceding to my wife the investigation of all bumps in the night, as I lay there useless and feeling like not much of a man.

Most fathers think about walking their daughters down the aisle. I only dreamed of walking mine back to bed.

On those nights my daughter came into our room, I would just lie there trying not to get emotional as my wife came to her aid. I was imprisoned in stony silence; the dead-beat dad unable to do any good.

I'd hear her yell, "Mommy!" and I'd simultaneously hope and dread that my name would come next. Such is the split-in-two life of the chronically ill: all of the perspective in the world, and the total inability to act on it.

Soon enough, "Mommy" was the only name Makena would call when she was scared.

Pre-surgery, this was my routine:

Bedtime typically came around 9:30, with me dressed in a sleek workout shirt and shorts. For Parkinson's patients, our sleeping hours require as much careful negotiation as our waking ones, and something as seemingly innocuous as a blanket can become a sarcophagus. I wore the silky clothes to eliminate as much friction as possible.

The night usually began pretty innocuously. The medication that kept my body limber was usually working when I climbed in bed, and I fell asleep within seconds of closing my eyes. Days spent in perpetual movement, followed by claustrophobic nights where I could not move at all, created a level of insane exhaustion. Before surgery, I went around four years without so much as one recuperative night's sleep. This is something they never tell you about chronic illness — that you can get to the point where you feel like you might drown in your own fatigue.

I'd sleep heavily for 2-3 hours, and then the dynamic part of my night would begin. By that point my medication would have completely worn off, with dystonia setting in as I laid there rigid as a plank, save for my arms shaking by my sides. In super-slow motion, I'd reach for an anti-anxiety pill on my nightstand, which I'd discovered through trial and error could sometimes relax me and my cramping muscles enough to get back to sleep.

Sometimes I'd fall back to sleep, but most of the time self-loathing would take its place. My mind would ping among scenarios in which I would be totally helpless: robber, earthquake, alien abduction... I'd lust for the chance to simply roll on my side, find the cool part of the mattress, and go to sleep. As it stood, I rarely used a blanket because of the potential for getting stuck inside it.

Sleep or no sleep, I was fully awake by 3 or 4 a.m. If I had to relieve myself, I'd roll/fall out of bed and crawl to the bathroom. The irony of this was constantly on my mind; that this body that had been my elevator to the highest heights now emasculated me to this degree. My toddler could walk herself to the bathroom, but I had to crawl; it was safer and quieter.

My brain was now turned on, with the Parkinson's following like a tail on a kite. The dystonia would set in again, this time curling my bare feet into little fists. Michael J. Fox taught me a trick to deal with this: put on your patent-leather dress shoes to make your feet lie flat. With that 10-minute task accomplished, my next destination was my recliner chair, a mere 100 feet and one mighty stairwell away.

Once safely down the steps, I'd pass by my office full of baseball memorabilia, including a sign that once hung in the Rockies weight room that reads, "The vision of a champion is someone who is bent over, drenched in sweat, at the point of exhaustion, when nobody else is watching." Yet there I stood with no one watching, feeling distinctly unlike a champion.

I'd fall like a tree in the forest into the recliner, inch my finger toward the remote control, and search for distraction until 6 a.m. when I could take my medicine, feeling it take effect in the toes of my left foot like the sun rising over a basin. I craved that sensation — an addict, for sure. The dyskinesia side effects would be along soon, my hands flailing, my head rolling around. The negotiations of the day would begin: tying my shoes, buttoning my shirt, getting a glass of water. But for those first few minutes when my two little pills would take hold, it was euphoric; a still-young man, sitting a room away from his baseball jerseys framed in glass, reveling in the wiggling of his toes.

Since my DBS surgery, I have improved enough that even when I'm off my medication, I am still able to walk around, get food and drinks, and do the little things my daughter might ask of me. But I hadn't had the chance to do the one thing I'd always wanted to.

On this particular night, I woke up and heard my daughter walking down the hallway. The sound of her footsteps sent me into action, as I'd rehearsed this event a million times in my head. I got up and walked to our door, where I met her with a "Shhhh." She had her little turtle nightlight, which was emitting tiny glowing spires that set off her sparkly Tinkerbell pajamas. Her hair was a massive confusion of yellow curls.

"What's wrong?" I asked.

"Can't sleep," she replied. "Just can't."

I stuck my hand out and took hers, escorting her back to her room.

I laid down with her, nose to nose. "Close your eyes," I said. "Try to go back to sleep with me."

She followed my example for about two minutes. Then for the next hour she tickled my face as I pretended to sleep.

I finally surrendered and made my 4:30 a.m. march downstairs, this time with her in my arms. We got some cereal, folded our bodies into my chair, watched "Tangled," and for two hours were a thicket of giggles.

There were many times that I resented the perspective Parkinson's gave me.

Now I'm thankful for it. There is no way I'd understand the awesomeness of a seemingly fractional moment like this one without the disease; without having my first DBS surgery fail to the extent that I almost lost it all.

A little over a year ago, through the fog of infection and a netherworld where I was more disease than man, I sent out tiny prayers to God like those streams of light from my daughter's toy, begging for one more chance to be this little girl's father.

I used to think that my being a champion depended on what I did when nobody else was watching. Now I know it's about what I'll do for this audience of one.

There we sat in our glowing house as night became day. I smoothed her hair. I smelled her neck. I heard her laugh. I closed my eyes.

And I said, "Thank you."

WE'LL BE FINE, I THINK

Dan Indante, Beverly Hills, CA

from *The Complete A**hole Dad*
Copyright 2014 Rare Bird Books. Reprinted with permission. Edited from original.

We have pretty traditional roles in our house. I go off to work every day and make the money; my wife stays home with the kids and bleeds me dry, all the while making it clear she does the real work.

Anyway, this was how it was when we first brought our daughter home from the hospital. It was July 2003. LA was undergoing a devastating heat wave and my wife's innards had been so shredded from pushing out our newborn bowling ball that she was literally on a catheter. Naturally, like my dad before me, I woke up on Day One, kissed the baby, and got the hell out of there.

I certainly spent my share of time with "Dan's Twin" (that's my kid, the one who's getting the other half of my wife's attention) at nights and on weekends, or whenever she was up for watching TV and sleeping. But if I was around the kid, my wife was somewhere around as well. I'm not gonna say she was scared to leave me alone with the baby but, if I'm being honest, she was absolutely terrified to leave me alone with the baby.

It's not that I was completely incompetent to care for a newborn child. I mean, I knew how to call 9-1-1 as long as the number was posted above the phone. I was aware she had a pediatrician. Somewhere.

Still, despite this myriad of parenting skills, my wife was hesitant to leave me alone with Dan's Twin. It couldn't last, however, and eventually she was going to get her bladder unhooked from the tube and go get a Slurpee or something.

I remember the day it finally happened, when she left me alone with our daughter. It wasn't some cataclysmic event like meeting the Dalai Lama or going out with the girls to get Cosmopolitans; she just wanted to go jogging. She was leaving so she could get skinny and be more attractive to me. I wasn't going to complain.

We were in the front room when my wife walked out in her jogging attire, sweat already forming on her upper lip, not from exercise, but from sheer panic.

"You sure you're going to be okay?" she said, shakily. Not exactly a ringing endorsement. "Yeah, we'll be fine," I said with a wave of my hand. I didn't mention I had my mom, my sister-in-law, a nanny, and a bonded day care facility all on red alert just in case. "OKAY," she said and slowly made her way out the door. I'm sure she assumed this was the last time she was ever going to see her daughter alive.

When the door closed behind her, my heart began racing. Jesus Christ, I didn't know what I was doing! I didn't know how to hold the kid or how to soothe her if she started crying. Hell, I barely knew her name.

Then she started whimpering slightly and, great, I thought, the first kid in history who will die of SIDS while her father is sitting right next to her. Turns out the dang binkie had just fallen out of her mouth. I shoved it back in with all the tenderness of an East German shot-putter and prayed to God she would fall asleep. I twitched every time I heard her make a noise. My heart rate shot above 200 when I didn't hear her make a noise. Somehow, notwithstanding the soothing environment of panic and hysteria that I created, Dan's Twin fell asleep before we got to ESPN's soccer highlights. I breathed a heavy sigh of relief and couldn't wait to down an entire bottle of 18-year-old Glenmorangie.

Forty-five minutes later, my sweating wife came home. She walked in the door, fully expecting me to confess to flushing the kid down the toilet or ironing her diaper instead of changing it. "How'd it go?" she asked, wincing while assuming the worst. "Huh," I responded with a snort, pretending I just woke up. "Did you leave?"

BEYOND THE AUTO-PILOT

Oren Miller, Owings Mill, MD

Thing is, we tried. We tried so hard. We had walked up and down the safety aisle at Toys'R'Us and bought everything we should ever need to make sure our kid would NEVER suffer an injury. Not on our watch! Unfortunately, kids are great at finding loop-holes, aren't they?

Neither my wife nor I do well in a crisis situation. I know some people chase these things like life is not worth living without a good crisis thrown in every now and then, but not us. We like things to go according to plan. Fortunately, between the two of us, someone usually manages to rise to the task, deal with the problem, and sit back down for the rest of the day, exhausted, while the other one lifts his or her head from the fetal position, making sure it's safe to get up.

When my wife went back to work and I started staying home with our boy, that luxury was over.

It was all up to me.

It was up to me when, as an infant, our boy somehow pulled himself up and fell from the crib. I called 9-1-1 for the first time in my life. It was up to me when he fell down the stairs and I rushed him to the doctor's office. It was up to me to deal with any crisis, and I realized I was doing OK, as long as the crisis involved an auto-pilot response.

But the older he got, the more complicated his injuries became. A doctor's visit, a hug, even a kiss on the booboo was no longer enough. His brain was getting too advanced for my brainless, auto-pilot, parenting style. One day, when he stuck his finger in a door and a piece of his skin was peeling off, I had to come up with something new.

First, I did the brainless, auto-pilot things. I took him to the bathroom and washed the blood off his finger. Then I put a Band-Aid on. Then I hugged him. Then I kissed him. Then I kissed his finger. Then I was out of ideas.

He was still crying, still in pain, and all I wanted to do was crawl into a safe corner and call my wife at work to come home and save us. Him first, I guess.

But when you decide to stay home with the kids, you have to step up. You don't have the option of regressing into an infant's state of mind when you take care of a child. You have to be an adult, which means that sometimes, when the auto-pilot is not enough and the solution will not come from outside, you have to improvise and search for an answer from within.

Here was a kid I loved. He was in pain. He was wearing a Band-Aid. The Band-Aid was plain. Think! THINK! And there it was! The answer! I quickly took out another Band-Aid and put it on my finger. I ran to the kitchen and got a Sharpie. I drew faces on both Band-Aids. Our fingers had faces, and they were going to go on adventures until my boy would stop crying!

It only took a few seconds. Sure, he was in pain, but he had better things to do than cry. After all, his finger had a face, and his dad's finger had a face, and the two fingers were now walking around, bumping into things, making funny noises, jumping, hitting each other...

Parenting is impossible without the auto-pilot. Sometimes, now with two kids, things get so hectic I find myself at night turning my brain on for the first time that day. Still, it's good to know we also have the capacity to "snap out" of it when we're most needed. I've made many mistakes as a dad, and many more will come, but I allow myself to be proud when I succeed. He's four now, and he can't remember that day, but I will always remember it. It was the day I fixed my son. The day I earned another notch on my Dad Badge.

FATHERING BLIND

Mike Heenan, San Mateo, CA

When I wasn't much older than my daughter is now, I was at my dad's house for one of our every-other-weekend visits. Wandering the daunting hallway one morning, I hung a sharp right and burst, unannounced, through the door to his bedroom. There he was, on his knees like I'd seen him before in the pews; only here his God was an all-white powder in a Tony Montana mini-mountain on the razor-strewn nightstand.

That wasn't my only memory of my father. He took me cat-fishing; the real kind. He took my cousin and I to the go-cart tracks to tear through the tire-lined course, lap after lap. He took me to see *Rocky IV* at the drive in and *The Last Starfighter* and lots of other places. I loved the man to death despite my mother's insistence he was "good for nothing."

I approached the task of becoming a father some three odd years ago eager, but basically flying blind. Where does the son of a deadbeat, or otherwise absent, dad look for a fathering model? What resource exists when you have hardly a single memory of how your father fathered you, save for some early outings and some later, concussive, head-butting? How do you know what to DO or DO DIFFERENTLY if you've never been exposed to how it's done? How do you handle fathering blind?

The prospect of becoming a father was petrifying.

After nine months spent worrying and waiting, my skyrocketing, white-knuckled fear of fatherhood reached its zenith on the day my daughter came into this world.

Sixteen long hours into my wife's guttural laboring, I too was steeped in sweat and letting unintelligible, senseless, sounds escape my face. I did my all to comfort her, to position her, to hold her, but the unbearable pain on her face was intensified by each new wince and assertion of her steely resolve. The panic-inducing vicissitudes of the torturous baby/mama heart monitor bottomed-out for the umpteenth time. Alarms started to sound and the vacuum of our birthing room was suddenly flooded with scurrying hospital workers. Phrases like "terminal emergency" and "trying too hard for too long" were tossed about by those in the know. I became even more terrified. Sheer panic gripped me as I watched my wife - my rock - getting strapped to a gurney and whisked off by a horde of doctors frantically trying to tie on surgical garb.

My memory gets foggy at this point, either a subconscious pain filter or an artifact of a past full of distances and substances. When I was finally tossed some scrubs and shoe covers, I was escorted to Emergency Surgery. The door opened to the set of a horror movie. I saw blood-soaked tables and tools. I saw mad scientists' bubbling beakers and bone saws and spools. I don't know what I saw, but I pulled myself together enough to go behind the partition to hold my wife's ghostly face and try to knead the fright from it. A few short moments later, and after whatever unthinkable things happened on the other side of that partition, I was called over to meet my daughter for the very first time.

There were no words to describe it. There was only a sense that is almost a sound. It was like the sound the Presto makes when my wife has finished cooking rice and twists the top-valve and the thick steam spews like Vesuvius and shoots to the ceiling. It was the sensation of a lifetime of fear and it's more recent evil twin, fear of fathering, flying from me the instant I pressed my daughter's face to mine. It was the monumental release when I cut the umbilical cord and ushered her into a world of wonder; a world we would occupy together for a while, hand in hand for as long as she'd have me, but certainly far longer than my father and I had. She was finally here and I was no longer afraid.

I realized I would only ever need her as my measuring stick. We would attempt, succeed and fail together in our respective roles, with nobody to tell us how it should be done, but, as I soon discovered, plenty of people out there who are willing to share their experiences with us. I would try not to dwell on my past, or other peoples' pasts. I needed only to look into her eyes to see we would share a roof and sing in the rain and pretend to visit uncharted planets and interpret their hieroglyphs.

My daughter is now three. She will not experience what I did as a child. I will give 100% of myself. Nothing is ever more important to me than being her dad and, because of her, I am no longer fathering blind.

PERFECT STRANGERS

Pat Jacobs, Elk Grove Village, IL

At 5 months, 4 days, 14 hours and 59 minutes into his short life, my child is going to be left alone with perfect strangers.

I decided I needed to hit the gym more regularly. Our gym has daycare for infants starting at six months, but my son is very mature for his age.

I enter the gym's Child's Play area sporting my spit-up-badge-of-fatherhood stain on my left shoulder. I act as calm as possible while I ask how this was supposed to work. If the kid cries for more than ten minutes, they will come find me. If he poops, they will come find me. If he starts gambling or writing Shakespeare, they will come find me. There is also a channel on the cardio equipment so I can watch him. I hand over my only child and begin to explain to the child care lady what he likes, what he doesn't like, how he can kind of sit up but it usually ends in a face-plant, if he cries, he likes to be on the left shoulder looking over your back... Then I realize she is looking at me like I was Balki Bartokomous from *Perfect Strangers*. I act cool when she asks if I am okay and give her my best Balki impersonation, "Don't be ridiculous!" I don't think she got it.

I calmly exit. Then I run to the locker room to put my stuff in the locker, run back into the gym area, go straight to a treadmill and look for the kid channel. It isn't there! I try another treadmill. Not there! I panic and head straight to the Child's Play area to cancel the whole deal but decide to stop and ask someone what channel it was on. Channel 21. Okay. Better. This should be posted everywhere; all over this damn gym for all of us who just want to stare at the screen and stalk our children! I punch in the numbers and paranoid parental relief is finally mine.

I stare at the kid channel. He seems all right. I start walking. They put him in a bouncy chair. Oh boy, this is bad. I force myself to look away from the screen, quickly look back at the screen, begin running. He seems okay. Stare at screen, stare at screen, BREATHE! At a quarter-mile, I see them put him into the crib and attend to other children. Oh boy, it is really bad. At a half-mile, people are looking his way. Oh boy, this is over. Someone walks over and picks him up. I pick up my pace. At three-quarters of a mile, it appears he is definitely crying hysterically, wondering why his father abandoned him. I pick up the pace even more. I haven't run this fast in my entire life, but I have to get this mile in. It is just one mile! I run as fast as I can, eyes glued to the screen. I finish the mile, world record time, gasping for air, jump off, run to the locker room, grab my stuff, sprint to the Child's Play area, swing open the door to rescue my child from the evil demons he thought were his new parents and… he is fine.

What happened to the screaming baby on the kid channel? Why doesn't this kid seem like he was being tortured? I smile, pick up my perfectly fine baby and ask the lady holding him if he was okay. She replies, "Don't be ridiculous," in a brilliant Balki impersonation.

Being a parent isn't easy and the mind plays tricks on you. I'm sure I'm not the first parent to have paranoid parental anxiety of leaving their little one with strangers for the first time. They, too, probably thought the worst was happening when, in actuality, everything was just fine. I'm not telling myself I need to get over all the little anxieties that are going to come along. I am telling myself that once it's over, I can laugh at the anxiety and realize, in the end, I'm a parent and I'm going to freak out. Even though I'm only a few short months in, I'm sure there will be many, many more times my brain plays tricks on me.

The question is: "In the end, will I come out just fine as a dad?"

Don't be ridiculous.

TAKING THE STAGE

Jason Ward, Benbrook, TX

I am not Super Dad. I don't own a World's Greatest Dad t-shirt. I am pretty certain I won't be getting any nominations for the Father of the Year Award. I am, however, a very good dad and I have been from the moment my wife and I heard the doctor say those words.... "Congratulations, you are going to have a baby." I am a firm believer my day-to-day involvement in my son's life is equally important as my wife's role as his mother. We both have demanding jobs, we both have equally busy lives, and we both invest every remaining moment into our family.

There are so many things for a child to learn in their early years: how to roll over, to crawl, to walk, to talk, to use the potty, to eat, to mind their manners, to stay in bed, tie their shoes, follow the rules, learn the A-B-Cs and 1-2-3s. I often think, "What if we've missed something? How is he going to succeed in life if I forget to teach him something important?"

But of all of life's lessons I know I'm responsible for as a parent, I feel most compelled to ensure I instill two things in my son: self-confidence and self-worth.

These are two things I struggled with throughout my own childhood. I was the tall, skinny kid with braces. I was shy and I was terrified to talk or perform in front of people and I missed out on a lot of fun stuff because of it. This pattern followed me into my adult years.

I think, as fathers, we all have a desire to give our best traits to our children and to shield them from our worst. Since his birth, I've had it in my mind that I did not want my son (who is now six-years-old) to inherit my lack of self-confidence. I wanted to give him the intrinsic tools he needed to live a different childhood than I had. But how do you give your child something that you do not possess? How do you teach something you don't understand?

I don't know if it was ever a conscious decision to try to change my own sense of self-confidence and self-worth, but when I became a father, something within me did change. I began challenging myself to step out of my hiding places and take on new things. I took on public speaking opportunities in my workplace. I followed a 20-year dream and learned to play guitar and to sing (out loud) in front of my wife, son, and friends. I organized a Dads Club in my son's elementary school to bring together fathers and their children. I'm not saying I am always comfortable doing these things, but I no longer let those discomforts keep me from being a good role model for my son. At six-years-old, he is not afraid to sing. He will take any opportunity to stand on stage. He aspires to be the leader every chance he gets and I can see these traits getting stronger in him every year. He is confident and you can see his sense of self-worth in his actions.

This story is not about my personal accomplishments and me. There really is a point to make here. I've learned you can teach lots of things to a child simply by repeatedly showing them the steps, but some things you can only teach by example. It's possible my son was just born with something I was not, but I like to believe that by overcoming my own limitations, I have instilled in him something that took me 35 years to find on my own. Someday when he is old enough to understand, I'm going to thank him for inspiring me to overcome... me.

A FATHER'S PLACE

Jeff Allanach, Frederick, MD

I loved riding my bike as a child. Feeling the wind through my hair as I pedaled my wiry legs gave me the first sense of freedom I can remember. I wanted my children to experience the same feeling, so I couldn't wait to teach my daughter, Celeste, how to ride a bike.

She had outgrown her bike with training wheels, so my wife and I decided to buy her a new bike for her 7th birthday. I took Celeste to the store and, as we walked the aisle looking for just the right bike, I told her I would not buy training wheels. The only way she would ride her new bike was if she let me teach her. She agreed.

We started on the driveway. I faced her as I straddled the front wheel and held the handlebars. I told her not to pedal, just let gravity take her down the incline. She lifted her feet off the ground, and I jumped back enough to let gravity catch her.

It worked.

Kind of.

She didn't fall, but she refused to go far down the driveway either. So I took her to the grass on the side of the house, figuring that falling on grass would hurt less than on the driveway. Holding the back of the seat and promising not to let go, I told Celeste I would run alongside her as she pedaled down the lawn. As it turned out, the lawn was too bumpy. A drunken Weeble Wobble had a better chance of balancing itself than Celeste had of riding her bike on the lawn.

We returned to the driveway, which she wouldn't leave for weeks. I felt defeated. She wouldn't let me take her beyond the driveway no matter how much I encouraged her.

She could see her friends riding their bikes without training wheels - some several years younger than she. I could tell she wanted to ride with them, but she still wouldn't let me teach her. So I stopped asking. I couldn't force her. She had to want to learn for herself. I didn't want her to forget about it either, so I hung her bike in the garage where she could see it as she climbed in and out of the car.

It hung untouched for 18 months.

Then one spring day, she asked me if I could teach her to ride her bike. She caught me off guard. I did not make a big deal out of it. I simply agreed.

We tried the driveway again which was met with as much success as before. Frustrated, she asked to try riding on the sidewalk a few houses away.

We stood at one end of the sidewalk. I told her I would run alongside her while holding the seat. She told me not to let go. I told her I might if I thought she could do it.

I could tell she was scared. I made her a promise: I would run alongside her and if she fell, she would fall into me (yeah, I didn't fully think that one through). She agreed. After several feet, I could feel her balancing on her own. I let go and ran alongside her. She stopped after 20 or 30 feet. I knelt down beside her, my hands embracing her waist.

"Sweetheart," I said nodding in the direction from which we came. "You see that tree down there? You rode all the way from there to here by yourself."

She stared at me in disbelief.

"I wasn't holding onto you that whole time. You were riding your bike all by yourself."

A smile grew and consumed her face, making her Christmas morning smiles look like smirks in comparison.

My eyes welled up for one of the few times in Celeste's life. Whenever I think of that moment, I can still see the pride on her face, and my eyes fill up. Her pride is contagious. I feel it because I taught her how to ride a bike, but quickly realize such pride is misplaced. I did not teach her to ride a bike. I was just running alongside her as she taught herself; the perfect place for a father to be.

GUILTY LOVE

John Pawlowski, Omaha, NE

I hate bedtime. It's as if my three kids have a not-so-secret pact to be as disobedient as possible and prolong the inevitable with wailing and gnashing of teeth. Often, they jump out of the bathtub to run around naked, hysterically laughing at their own poop jokes until I tackle and pin them to the floor, shoving tiny squirming feet into footie pj's they outgrew a year ago ("No, they're fine," I insist to my wife when she suggests again that we cough up the $5 to buy new pajamas). I do my best to chalk it up to "comes with the age territory" as my children are ages six, four, and two (girl, boy, girl), but I have to admit, those 30-45 minutes drains every last ounce of goodwill from my body.

It was after such a wrestling match one evening that my dad sense alerted me to the fact that my eldest daughter had opened her bedroom door and was creeping around upstairs after she had already been sung a song and tucked into bed. It was a clear violation of Dad Law all over the world. This was now "me time" and my relaxing TV shows weren't going to watch themselves.

"GET BACK INTO YOUR ROOM AND SHUT THE DOOR," I roared. The creeping noises instantly stopped and moments later, I heard her door softly click shut. I settled back into my couch throne, smug in my masculinity and disciplinarian prowess. At least my kids knew "the voice" and when it was time to get serious about obeying.

Two hours later, my wife and I made our way to our upstairs bedroom, pausing at each of the kids' rooms to tuck them in one last time and turn off the lights. As we reached our room, I noticed something on my pillow. I knew from a quick sidelong glance at my wife that she was equally perplexed. As I neared my side of the bed, I realized the item was a small, handwritten note from my eldest daughter with a piece of her Valentine's Day candy attached to it. The note simply read, "I love you Daddy." I knew two facts instantaneously: 1) I had one of the sweetest daughters on the planet, and 2) I had crushed her heart when I yelled at her hallway creeping which had clearly been to perform this clandestine turndown service. My sweet soul mate looked at me and righteously indicted, "I think you owe her a big apology tomorrow."

Saying sorry wouldn't have been enough. My daughter had given selflessly of herself the best way she knew how. I needed to return the gesture in kind. Memories are tender and fickle creatures; one never knows what will be remembered years later. I desperately wanted to overwhelm the negative I had caused with something positive. A few days later, on a normal work weekday, I announced to my boss and colleagues I had an important engagement. I left for lunch and didn't return. I drove home, picked up my Kindergartner and informed her the rest of the day was going to be a daddy/daughter date. I told her she could choose whatever she wanted us to do. Seeing her face light up properly erased the guilty millstone that had been hanging around my neck.

We spent the next five hours chumming around having fun by eating out, seeing a movie in the theater, washing the car and riding our bikes. It struck me as we ate our lunch together that I am often too focused on *teaching* my children (a correct and worthwhile endeavor if ever there was one). I also realized I need to build in some time to *love* my children. And so I told my daughter how special it was to have received the affectionate note from her the other night. I explained how daddies sometimes don't say the right things at the right time, but she made each day of my life better by having her in it. If you're also a dad reading this who has ever made a similar comment to his daughter, I hope you'll understand my feeble attempt to explain the radiance I saw emanating from her face as she bashfully took another bite of her sandwich and then snuggled in next to my side. That's what good parenting feels like. I was both shocked and emboldened by the observation that I hadn't felt it nearly enough in recent months.

My one regret in this story is that my action taken was fueled by guilt and not by a more benevolent reason. With this great experience under my belt, however, I'll be looking to do a little less lecturing and a lot more loving on a consistent basis.

LIVING FOR FATHERHOOD

Ryan E. Hamilton, Gaithersburg, MD

During the day, I work. At night, I work. And at all times of the day, I parent.

I have a fast-paced tech career in the mobile advertising industry. I write massive amounts of code and construct mobile ads for many top brands. In addition to my ad agency day job, I run several entrepreneurial ventures. One of my moonlighting duties is running a successful health, wellness and nutrition site with my college buddies. Another is developing a popular social network and entertainment destination for fathers.

Most importantly, I'm a father to a wonderful seven-year-old son with Autism and ADHD. He needs to be shuttled to and from school, play date appearances, and countless therapy sessions. He requires help with his homework. He asks for my support for basic and intermediate executive functioning skills. He wants me to teach him how to code so he can grow up to be a game developer. He needs me to cook for him or grab a burrito at the local Mexican grill. He begs me to play video games with him throughout it all.

I'm also in the midst of a contentious divorce with my son's mother, a situation that does not bode well in the alleviation of life's stress.

An outsider would think I'm busy as hell, way overextended, ready to throw in the towel.

I'm busy in the strictest definition of the term. But I embrace it all. In fact, I love it.

My life is full, but I'm enriched by it.

Three years ago, however, I did not feel this way about my life. I was extremely depressed, on the brink of suicide.

My wife moved out of the house and took all of our possessions across the country to begin a happier life without me. She took our [then] four-year-old son with her, leaving me in an empty home with no furnishings, no family or loved ones, surrounded only by houseplants.

A few months later, I got laid off from my full-time job. This sent my life spiraling down even further. I was on the verge of emotional and financial collapse.

During my darkest times, I drank six-packs of beer, ate hoagies and bags of potato chips from local convenience stores in a futile attempt at good health and spirit.

I thought a lot about my son in those times. I realized I needed to be there for him no matter what happened between his mom and me. That epiphany gave me the strength to avoid giving up hope for a better life.

I also had a great creative outlet: I wrote code around the clock. The code I wrote back then turned into Life of Dad, an incredible social network for dads. Its success has given me hope for the future, and a sense that my life matters.

Today I have what I feel is a dream job for me. I work from home, with freedom and flexibility to balance most of life's demands. While I have plenty of deliverables and deadlines, all due yesterday (at worst) and ASAP (at best), I love every last moment of it.

While people are fighting traffic, skipping morning workouts and scarfing down breakfast wraps just to clock into jobs they barely endure, I'm taking a leisurely stroll to my local Whole Foods store or farmer's market to select my produce for the day.

Yes, I shop for fresh produce daily. I prepare every meal from scratch. I chop fruits, I cut vegetables, I mince roots and herbs, I sprinkle spices, I smash avocados, I crack organic pepper, I stir dressings, I tear apart leafy greens....

In the midst of all the stuff I've got going on, I make it a point to treat myself right.

I used to think my destination in life was so important that the place I had to be at any given moment was far more important than the place I was in at that moment.

It's not.

What I discovered was I don't have to do anything in this life. Absolutely nothing. I don't have to be anywhere. I don't have to be anywhere ON TIME. I don't have to work. I don't have to make money. I don't have to have things. I don't have to report to a boss. I don't have to commit or over commit to anything.

When I decided not to kill myself three years ago, it was an ever-so-slight assertion to myself and to the world that my life mattered, even if in a small way. I had a son depending on me. I had friends and business partners who believed enough in me to trust me with delivering their ideas and dreams. I also began to believe I could be of service to others and make a positive difference. So, I decided to live.

I remember telling myself, "If life is gonna suck this hard, I might as well do what I love." From that point forward, I guarded my time against those who would demand it and mistreat it. I focused on my passion.

I see people stressed out and sleep-deprived by all of the busyness in their lives and the demands and tasks of today. I look at them and I see my former, suicidal self.

I don't tell them to change their ways. I'm not sure they'd listen, let alone understand. However, I do wish them well.

People often ask me, "Ryan, how the heck do you do it all?"

"I don't."

THE PLACES MY MIND GOES

Lorne Jaffe, Douglaston, NY

I've been suicidal a number of times throughout my life, but I've never had a serious plan (outside of downing a bottle of sleeping pills) or written a note. I never had the courage to go through with it (and yes, though it's a selfish act, it does take bravery to actually do it, in my opinion). At best, I'd imagine I was like Huck Finn, watching his own funeral. At worst, I imagined holding the bottle of pills. I hadn't thought about offing myself since long before Elaine, my wife, became pregnant. At least three years. Then, suddenly, the thought returned.

The moment began after waking from a nightmare sometime after 3 a.m. I couldn't remember what it was about, but it doesn't matter. I'd been anxious all day about my blog. I hadn't written in more than a week. There were a slew of ideas in my head, but I couldn't seem to write any of them.

I was awake and frazzled so I decided to check Facebook on my phone to get my mind off my anxiety. Big mistake.

I read blog posts from my fellow dad bloggers. My chest began hurting. I'm not good enough, I thought. These guys are so much better than me. They keep pumping out words, heartfelt, poetic words. I'll never be a real writer.

I saw pictures of decorated houses. The thought occurred to me that I'll never own a home. Sienna, my daughter, will never have a backyard in which to play, to build snowmen like in some of those pictures.

Negative thoughts attacked like rebellious white blood cells. I'm a failure. I was supposed to *be* something! I was supposed to have a prestigious job and money! I was supposed to be a success! Friends from grade school have houses! And they're rich! I'm going to be 40 in a couple of months and I've accomplished NOTHING! Just end it already!

Rationality was out the window. My chest felt like cement.

I went from anxiety about what to write on my blog to suicide in just a few seconds.

My thoughts scared the hell out of me, but they refused to abate. I lay in bed shaking.

I can't kill myself because of Elaine and my daughter Sienna. I can't do that to them. Wake Elaine up! Wake her up and tell her what was going on! Have her hold you. Calm you. But I couldn't. She needed to sleep so she could function at work.

Trembling, I dropped my phone and clung to Elaine hoping she'd feel me and wake up, but I still couldn't allow myself to actually awaken her. I started hyperventilating.

Breathe! Breathe! Breathe!

I tumbled out of bed and dizzily walked down the hall, my thoughts still racing.

Go into Sienna's room and watch her. It'll help. No. I'll wake her up. Can't do that. Find the cat. Find Minky.

"Minky," I whisper, voice hitching. "Minky."

I found the puffball in the closet. I grabbed and held him so tightly he squeaked. I took him back to the bedroom, concentrating on his purring. He climbed onto my aching chest, his purr like a chainsaw. He nosed my face, licked my hand. I gently stroked him, feeling the softness of his fur. I scratched him behind his ears. Over and over I pet him. But still the negative thoughts attacked.

FAILURE! How can you think of suicide? How could you do that to your family? SHUT UP, BRAIN! SHUT UP, SHUT UP!

I pet Minky for more than an hour, depressed, shivering, using all my power to concentrate on what was right in front of me. 5 a.m. passed. Elaine still slept peacefully, totally unaware of the storm raging beside her. Finally, I joined her but it was a restless sleep; the type of fitful doze where you hover between wakefulness and dreaming.

My alarm woke me at 8. I hit the snooze button a few times because I wasn't ready to deal with the day – having to put on a brave face while playing with and teaching a rambunctious toddler.

When I finally got out of bed around 8:30, I struggled down the hall to the kitchen, lower-body leaden, head filled with helium, stomach churning, an invisible anvil squashing my chest. Shell-shocked, I moved like something out of *The Walking Dead*.

Suicide? Do I still hate myself that much?

I gave Sienna breakfast, but had nothing myself. The meal was nearly silent on my part unlike most days when I sing her favorites whether it be "C is for Cookie" or the theme from *The Golden Girls* (no idea why, but she loves it). After breakfast, I set Sienna down in her playpen so I could shower and do the dishes as I do every morning. I had the shakes in the shower but recovered. We spent the morning playing with cars and stuffed animals while I watched the clock, begging for the hours, minutes, and seconds to pass so I could put her down for a nap and perhaps conk out myself.

At one point I dragged myself to the computer and wrote this on Facebook: "Very depressed. Doing my best trying to hold it together for Sienna." I then shut the computer wondering why I did that fully believing no one would care.

Soon afterwards, my mom texted me to say she'd read my Facebook post and asked if I needed help. I mentioned I'd appreciate it if she'd give Sienna dinner – just the thought of putting together a meal and getting her to eat was too much for me to bear. My mom agreed to come over even though she had a cold leaving me to imagine Sienna getting sick as my punishment for being so pathetic.

I don't remember much of the afternoon. I'm sure I followed Sienna around whenever she grabbed my hand and commanded me to sit so she could show me something or we could play. I struggled to smile. I kissed and hugged her when I could gather the strength to do so. I couldn't wait to put her to bed.

Was I asleep when my mom rang the bell at 5:30? Was Sienna still in her crib talking to herself in the dark? I can't recollect. I sat on the couch staring into space while my mom fed my daughter eggplant rollatini. She brought me a salad which I eventually ate, the first food I'd had all day. My mom tried to get me to talk, but I couldn't. I mumbled. I spoke in short sentences. I didn't mention suicide despite the flashing neon sign in my mind.

After dinner, my mom stayed with us. I went to change the cat litter and it was like a perfect storm. We have one of those cat litter boxes that you roll over to get the clumps out, but it picked this time - THIS TIME - to fall apart leading to urine-infused litter spilling all over the kitchen floor. Immediately, I couldn't breathe. My facial tic (a remnant from my breakdown four years prior) spasmed like crazy. Sienna kept coming into the kitchen and I stuttered, "Sie-Sie-Sienna ou-ou-out!" I cleaned up the mess on the verge of both tears and my second panic attack in less than 15 hours. My mom hugged me when I finished cleaning. Did I hug her back? I don't think so. I think I was like a rag doll.

I returned to the couch. Sienna picked up ribbons and Mardi Gras-type beads and wanted me to spin and shake them. She climbed on my lap. Minky, the intuitive black, long-haired puffball, curled up next to me and purred. I kissed Sienna's head while petting Minky, his purr rumbling against my thigh. I still had that 100-yard stare, but my mom observed something else and later wrote in an email:

"After you threw away the cat litter and barely made it back to the couch, your beautiful, wonderful daughter took one look at you and with all the love in her heart climbed in to your lap and cuddled with you. And while fighting through your embarrassment of having her see you this way (yes, I saw that too), she held firm and would not let her daddy go. Tell the world how you both looked at each other and ever so slowly she was able to calm you down (with a little help from a purring Minky) until the softness showed in your face and you were able to begin to play with her. She only had her daddy in her eyes and I watched as the two of you played with the ribbons over and over again and pure glee showed in Sienna's face and smiles came in to your face. It was a beautiful moment between father and daughter. She was there for you all the way and while you were not free of all the anxiety and panic, she helped you hold it together. And because of her, you fight on. You were given the powerful gift of pure, unadulterated love yesterday while you were most vulnerable. That is what it is all about. How amazing that a 21-month-old has such a gift. That is the perk of being able to share these moments with her. That is something the world and all the stay-at-home dads need to know."

I wish I remembered things in this manner. I remember Sienna in my lap. I remember Minky. I remember playing with ribbons. I don't remember my face softening or my brain unlocking or an ease coming over me. All I have are my mom's words. She was right. The unequivocal father-daughter bond must have been present allowing me to keep fighting despite my extreme fears and vulnerability. And though the events my mom witnessed are foggy in my mind, as is my collapsing into Elaine's arms when she got home and my nightmarish confession about my suicidal thoughts, I CLEARLY remember the following morning when I had a phone therapy session and Sienna, a toddler bursting with energy, sat on my lap for 20 minutes as my tears dripped in her hair and Minky, perceptive Minky, curled up next to me and purred.

I don't know when exactly I crossed the line into feeling better, but I do know the words of encouragement from fellow dad bloggers, the emails and phone calls from friends and family, and the unburdening in therapy (I think I spent most of the time crying and repeating my usual "I don't understand" and "I'm trying so hard" and "When will it stop?" refrains as my therapist pointed out how much I'd accomplished over the past few years), did help.

I don't know when I'm going to suffer another panic attack. With depression, you're never out of the woods. There are so many triggers and dangerous thoughts that zip through my brain each and every second that anything can set me off at any time.

But I do know I have people who care about me (I still struggle to understand why – I wish I could just accept it) and I have my blog, my own words to read and reread as proof that I'm gradually moving down the right path.

I know I'm going to face anxiety again. I can't avoid it. But I also know there are people out there who support me even though I've never even met some of them.

Most of all, though, I have my little family – an incredible wife, a brilliant, funny, beautiful little girl who gives me "the powerful gift of pure, unadulterated love" and our two cats, one of which always knows when I'm hurting.

And, as my mom so aptly wrote: that's what it's all about.

PART FOUR

FATHERHOOD AT WORK

"I am the father, the discipliner, the teacher, the brick wall, the soft jelly, the sensitive one, the insensitive one, the mediator, the chauffeur, the over-protective one, the naysayer, the explainer, the answer man, the hated one, the comforter, the movie goer, the boyfriend watcher, and the boyfriend warner."
- *Bob Boisvert, father of 3 daughters in Largo, FL*

ROCKING MORNINGS

Shannon Carpenter, Lee's Summit, MO

3
......
2......
1......

Boom!

The screaming is loud and shrewd; it cuts through the air darting and jabbing into my brain. It coincides with the big toe jabbing me in the back of the calf.

I'm not sure why my wife decides to communicate with the big toe - that one is still a mystery. She at least has the ability to have loving conversations with me. I have accepted the big toe as part of the marriage. Perhaps it's her direct nature and the big toe communication is effective.

I roll out of bed and take stock of myself. I am alive. I have a great wife, despite her big toe communication network. I have three great children; they just happen to be loud and rise almost as soon as I put them to bed. My knees still work and my beard doesn't have any glue in it from a school project completed the previous day. I take a deep breath, gather my thoughts and begin my day the only way I know how. It's time to unleash the awesome.

I grab my boy, Ollie, 10 months of poop and vinegar. We head downstairs while dodging cat puke and two very excited dogs who try to trip me. The baby goes in the high chair. I throw Cheerios at him. He likes them and more importantly the dogs like them which is good because in about five minutes they will end up on the floor. I let the dogs out and manage to remember my boots before I step into the snow on the back porch. You only make that mistake once, my friends.

I make a bottle and hand it to the boy at about the same time the last of the Cheerios hit the floor. I hear the dogs barking in the back yard. They are ready to come in. They have Cheerios on the brain and the thought of those delicious morsels just sitting on the floor must drive them crazy. I'm like that with Big Macs.

Now is my quiet time. It's the only quiet time I will have for the next several hours. This is my time to check the news, perhaps play a little iPhone game, contact the President of Uganda and ask about the conditions in that part of the world. It's not much - about 30 minutes - but I don't think I could make it without these 30 minutes; these sweet wonderful 30 minutes.

The other kids are awake. Time to get everyone rolling.

Like Tarzan calling for his jungle friends, I yell upstairs. It's almost a yodel with a deep bass signifying that for all that is holy you don't want me to come up there to get you because if I do go up there, I'm bringing a bucket of ice water and a rabid baboon. I'll throw both in your room, shut the door and whatever comes out later gets some bacon.

As the rest of my kids are crawling out of bed, I turn on the tunes. I don't choose easy listening songs in the morning; that's not our style. We are not an easy listening family. We are a family in constant motion. I put on Metallica, perhaps some Rage against the Machine. Loud and proud! Shock and awe: that's our mornings. I can't afford to have my kids sluggish; they won't get anything ready for school. As it stands, they don't much now.

The older two plow downstairs like elephants doing jumping jacks. They are not gentle, they are not quiet; they are an air horn with its button stuck. I get them to the table in time to sometimes catch the bottle my 10-month old hurls at the dogs. It's a game we play called "God Damnit". He wins almost every time.

Younger, earlier on as an at-home dad, I imagined myself creating masterpiece omelets, pancakes that practically flipped themselves, quiches that were divine. But as it turns out, kids don't care much for quiche and I've found that pancakes on a school morning is generally about as good an idea as chocolate syrup in Froot Loops. The requests I'm willing to take: awesome omelets, scrambled eggs and bacon, a number 12 hold the mayo, bring the hash, never come. One wants cereal, the other wants cinnamon toast. I add some oranges, fresh cut up melon, maybe even a side of bacon because bacon is awesome.

I bring the food to the table reminding the kids not to get any food on their blankets. Yup, they bring blankets to the table and I allow it. Why? Because blankets are about as awesome as bacon, that's why. The baby gets melon and oranges. He'll actually eat half of that before throwing it at the dogs. I do it while rocking out because rocking out is happy time.

Our rocking morning sets the right tone for the day. We are going to conquer this day. We are going to grab it by the scruff of the neck and force it to be awesome. We are going to have a happy morning. We have problems, we all have problems, but we are going to face them as a family and kick them in the teeth. That's my real job in the morning: setting the right attitude for the day, and it's more important than just about anything else combined. Spelling test today? Own it. Sight words this afternoon? Conquer them and make them watch as you pillage their village.

The kids finish breakfast and head to the couch. They want to watch cartoons and I generally let them because I'm busy changing the baby and the poop bomb he has conjured this morning. Seriously kid, what the hell? You don't eat enough to even make such monstrous poop bombs.

I send the other two kids up to get dressed for school. I let them pick out what they want to wear just because I do so love the argument that will soon follow. My daughter has caught on and now wears mostly appropriate clothing, such as shorts and short-sleeved shirts in the middle of winter. I rarely even look up anymore to check her outfit; I just tell her to change it. I like my odds of being right. My son somehow finds shirts that he wore three years ago and states it fits fine, it's his favorite shirt, dad please oh please oh please. I let him get the second please out before sending him back up. This is all highly coordinated because I do need the extra time to figure out which room the cat has been locked in by the now mobile baby. If I don't let him out soon, he'll crap a tornado and I deal with enough poop in my normal routine that I really try to avoid any poop extra credit.

The kids arrive downstairs dressed. I remind my daughter to brush her hair or else I will do it. There is no argument from her. I have big sausage finger hands that were not made for delicate work. For much of her life, my hands, trying to be gentle as they possibly could, mangled her head when I brushed it. My daughter quickly learned to brush her hair.

I tell my son to find his shoes. He slowly turns in a circle in the middle of the living room looking at his feet, shocked they aren't already on there, those bastards. "Dad, I can't find my shoes," he says. I remind him, like I do every morning, that they are in the shoe basket, where they have been every day for the last three years. He finds them as my daughter finishes her hair and he begins to put the shoes on. He does this while hanging upside down.

I start making lunches. The baby doesn't like when I stand at the counter, I don't know why. He head butts my leg and half the time, he knocks himself a little silly on my shin. He falls then stares up at me like it's my fault.

Lunches packed and in the backpacks. I take this opportunity to go through the backpacks and pull out anything the two older kids have forgotten to give me the day before, such as notices of plays, homework assignments, or that it's their turn to bring snacks.

Finally, I throw the jackets and gloves at the children. I make them put them on ten minutes prior to the bus arriving because if you don't, they will "forget" and then you are trying to get it done running to the bus stop while carrying a baby through snow. It's not fun. I don't recommend it.

I turn off the music and finally sit down right about the time my wife comes down from her hour long ritual of getting ready for work. In her eyes, we look peaceful, complete and somewhat lazy. The kids are ready to go, permission slips for girl scouts are signed and there is usually a bagel waiting for her. And more often than not, her lunch is packed on the counter next to her purse, computer and car keys.

She sees me yawn as I sit in my chair; my sweet blissful chair. "What on earth do you do in the morning?" she asks me.

FLYING SOLO

Jim Chapa, Downers Grove, IL

I arrive at Cleveland Hopkins Airport with my two-and-a-half year-old daughter and my ten-month-old son in tow. Every parent (and for that matter, everybody who's ever flown) dreads flying with an infant or toddler. I am about to attempt both. Solo.

A scheduling necessity had placed my wife in Chicago, 350 miles away, on a cold, snowy winter evening. As a family, we are experienced air travelers, but this was not a divide and conquer event. I am, literally, flying solo.

The crumb-crunchers and I arrive at our gate on time without incident; no minor accomplishment I might add. Bags are checked, stroller ready to be gate-checked. The diaper bag is stocked, formula bottles locked and loaded.

Our flight is on time, all systems: go! Only then do I realize our flight is on a small puddle jumper, leaving from the tarmac level. No problem, I think to myself. "I'll carry Patrick and hold Kayla's hand."

The three of us slowly climb down the stairwell, one exciting, adventurous step at a time. Out into the light snow, we meander over to the plane. Lots and lots of scary noises are out here, and I can feel Patrick's grip tighten around my neck. Kayla is wide-eyed and suddenly hesitant. As we approach the plane, we see a mountain of open and rickety looking steps that my daughter refuses to climb. Suddenly, my fearless companion of the past two years is not feeling it. I remind myself she's not being irrational. She is being two.

Now what?

I drop the diaper bag, asking Kayla to hold onto the strap for me (giving her something to do), bound up the stairs and hand Patrick to the startled stewardess at the top. Before she or my son can protest, I race back down, fling the diaper bag over my shoulder, hoist Kayla, and carry her up the stairs. I set her down, retrieve Patrick, and we're on board! I grab the first two seats I see, in an attempt not to hold things up for my fellow passengers, who've been watching in what I imagine to be a mixture of amusement and terror.

That wasn't so bad.

Not until I'm settled in do I remember that we're NOT flying Southwest, and random seating is not really an option. We have assigned seats somewhere. As I ponder this, calculating the amount of repacking I need to do, a serious business-looking type comes down the aisle.

He looks at his ticket, then at us, then back at his ticket. I show him the ticket to my true seat, ten aisles away, "This is where we're supposed to…" and he's gone before I finish my sentence.

My aisle-mate watches him go, possibly with envy. I expertly entertain my kids until we hit the runway, settle my daughter in with her Winnie-the-Pooh blanket, pull out the "take-off" bottle and plug Patrick in. Soon we're at thirty thousand feet, and the important ones are sleeping. The look on the stewardess's face as she comes down the aisle is priceless.

On to the home stretch!

Although any parent is reluctant to wake a sleeping baby, I know from experience my kids need to be vigorously working on something in their mouths as we descend, or else screams of ear-popping agony will occur. The woman across the aisle looks on in astonishment as I gently shake my sleeping children awake. Bracing myself for the worst, the landing is quiet and uneventful. As the "fasten your seatbelt" signal chimes and turns off, I get the feeling there will be high-fives all around, if I had a hand to spare.

I'm certainly ready to declare "mission accomplished" as we file off the plane. Meeting my anxious wife at the gate, I'm not sure which of the four of us was the happiest, but I know dad delivered.

ATTACK OF THE ZOMBIE BABY

James Kline, Apex, NC

It" happened one random night and remains one of my hardest moments as a new stay-at-home father.

Our son was only six-months-old at the time and, so far, a great sleeper. It was just past midnight (only twenty minutes after I laid my own head down) when he startled us awake with a loud cry. This cry was different; not of pain, hunger or fright, but a cyclical cry/whine/whimper. I silenced the monitor and dashed upstairs to investigate. It only took a few minutes for me to realize something was up, something different, something out-of-the-norm with my son.

I left the lights off for a few minutes and observed before getting involved. Was he sleep-crying? A bad dream? I have nightmares - terrible ones in fact - but what could a six-month-old possibly be scared of? A breast-milk shortage? Joking aside, I became very concerned when he wouldn't respond to my voice. I turned the lights on and tried soothing actions such as rubbing his belly which worked like a charm on many previous nights. Then I started clapping my hands, trying to get his attention. His eyes opened, but he did not seem to see me. He looked like a zombie. I picked him up, cradled him in my arms and walked around. He was not alert or aware, but appeared awake. We moved to different rooms in the house; we even went outside for some brisk air but nothing calmed him down. I could not console my son!

I grabbed bunny (a favorite toy hiding in the laundry basket). He helped a bit, but the cyclical crying continued. After nearly an hour of walking and rocking and humming, he suddenly came out of it and fell asleep. I imagine he was completely exhausted. I was. I placed him back in the crib, rubbed his belly for a few minutes while he fell asleep like nothing happened. I never felt so helpless in my life.

Totally baffled, and energized by both mystery and fear, I immediately did an internet search. Yes, I know, internet searches at 2am about medical or sleep issues will generally make a bad thing worse. In this case, I found a resource that eased my mind and helped solve the mystery. My son experienced "night terrors". Wow... (exhale) I must have missed that section in the "new parent brochure".

Night terrors, I learned, are an interruption in a child's REM sleep. It is not uncommon for a growing baby brain, especially one learning to sleep and dream. A combination of illness and lack of sleep can trigger this in children of all ages. I also learned that over-stimulation after it occurs only makes it worse. I wish I had known that a few hours before! After another hour of internet research, I discovered my son was never really awake; he was stuck between sleep stages.

I found my way back to the comfort of my own bed, turned the monitor on and prayed it would not happen again. As I shut my eyes, all I could hear was his cyclical, hysterical screaming and crying in my head. I can still hear it.

The next day, my wife and I discussed what happened. Looking back, our son did run a slight fever and was transitioning from three to two naps per day. Both, as it turned out, were contributing factors to the night terror episode. Picking him up and turning on the lights only perpetuated it.

There are differing philosophies on how to handle night terrors. Some parents will pick up their baby, some will let their baby cry it out. I had no idea what was happening, so I picked him up. We decided if it happened again, we would watch him through the monitor, since my efforts did not seem to help. Luckily, over the next few nights, he slept well.

Three months later, when my wife was several states away on business, "it" happened again. I immediately recognized the crying, as if it happened only yesterday. This time, there were no obvious triggers, no sleep issues, no illness. As I watched him via the monitor, I noticed he was playing with his crib-mounted aquarium (a new favorite bedtime toy). He was acting like a zombie again, hitting the toy, setting off the lights and music, then crawling around the crib crying. He would lay down for a minute, then pop back up and hit the aquarium again. This went on for 15-20 minutes before I decided to intervene. I realized this toy was over-stimulating him during his "stuck REM cycle" and perpetuating more night terrors.

I flew up the stairs with a mission - stop the zombie baby! Once in his room, I had to get this toy out of the crib. Easier said than done, as it was both strapped and tied along the back side of his crib. I thought, "This is really going to mess him up," but it had to be done. After I chucked the toy into another room, I killed the lights, picked him up and held him close while I rocked in the chair. After twenty minutes of rocking and humming tunes from The Doors (see, dads are cool), he was sleeping in my arms. "Success! I am the greatest dad alive," I thought to myself and gently put him back down in his crib. Of course it was not quite that easy, as it took one more round of rocking and humming to ensure he was down for the night.

I believe it is important for every parent to be aware of his child's emotions, schedules and reactions. My instincts told me something was off. I tried several things. I did research. I talked to my wife. Even if it was out of my comfort zone, I knew I had to find a solution that would work for my son.

Thankfully, my son no longer has night terror issues. We now have a daughter, who just turned six months old, but if she has "it", I'll know what to do.

BIG HEART

J. Adam Lowe, Cleveland, TN

I believe at the heart of being neighborly, friendly, and influential is an understanding of how to be empathetic toward others. It is not enough to recognize other's needs but to also understand the power of their emotions and situation. This is a lesson that organically arrived to my son at five, an age that may be considered too soon.

It is not at all uncommon for my son to come zipping into a room, ready to share some new excitement, some crowning achievement, or even a recently fabricated joke. This time was no different. I could hear the "Blaine train" coming from a room away, his feet thumping the hardwood as a rhythm to the tune of "Daddy! Guess what?!"

"What is it son?" I asked.

"Why don't animals take tests?" he posed with the anticipatory look in his eye, ready to burst with the answer regardless of my response.

"I don't know. Why don't you tell me?" I replied.

Suddenly, the excitement in his face drained away. His eyes had shifted from me to the television. His expression moved from joyful exuberance to troubled.

In the middle of his joke, my son was taken in by a commercial on television displaying the plight of children in foreign countries. He was captured by the image of a malnourished little boy staring blankly at the camera. He was confused, yet moved, by the comments of the narrator as he explained many children had no parents to look after them.

"Blaine, are you okay?" I asked as I touched his arm.

"Why don't that boy have parents?" he responded with a mix of sadness and anger.

"Well, I'm not sure but some kids don't have parents because they may be sick, have passed away or even run away," I answered.

"Some parents run away?! But why don't they feed that little boy?" he continued, his expression growing ever more angry.

"Yes, some parents do run away but you see those other people, those other adults there? They are working hard to help that little boy and love him," I explained as I pulled him into my lap.

I knew the intricacies of inequity were too heavy for any five-year-old but I also knew my son. He would not relent until he felt he understood. He had a spirit of determination that demanded answers and I knew I couldn't dodge this situation with the ole' "you'll understand when you're older" response.

"Blaine, seeing that little boy makes you sad doesn't it?" I posed as I began to redirect the conversation.

He nodded in agreement.

"First, I want you to know that you are very lucky because you have a momma and daddy who love you. Not only that," I continued, "but you have grandparents and aunts and uncles and all kinds of people who will always make sure you are okay. Also, I am proud of you. You have a big heart and when people have big hearts, they are concerned for others. I have always prayed you and your brother and sister would have big hearts. It takes a big heart to do big, difficult things. Those people on the TV who are helping those kids have big hearts too."

"I want to help that boy," Blaine said, finally turning his attention away from the television as the commercial ended.

"I know you do and we help people like him all the time. Do you remember the boxes we made at Christmas?" I quizzed.

"Yes," he replied.

"Do you remember when we took a bunch of your toys to another family?" I asked again.

"Yes," he replied.

"And do you remember all the times Daddy has talked to you about helping those who aren't as strong or fortunate as you?" I asked.

"Yes," he replied.

"We do all these things to help others," I explained. "We help feed people who are hungry and we help make kids happy with toys because we are able to help. We use our ability and our big hearts to make a difference. We may not be able to go across the world to help that boy but we can help kids just like him around here. And we do. You do."

"I'm glad we help people," he revealed as I saw the smile return to his face.

"Me too, Buddy. Now, why don't animals take tests?" I asked with a sincere desire to hear his punch line.

"It's because there are too many cheetahs!" he answered with all the excitement returning to his face.

I will admit I was intimidated by this situation. With my son so emotionally primed, I knew it wasn't an opportunity I could let pass. Despite my own fear and uncertainty, I chose to reinforce something my son had already known. In a subject matter that was too mature for his age, I gave context he could understand. I will never forget the moment and I am sure there are more in store.

BOOBY TRAP

Kevin McKeever, Stamford, CT

Some claim that I, a straight American male, am biologically hard-wired to notice breasts. I won't argue with science, unless the breasts in question belong to my pre-teen daughter.

Just the other day there she was: a sweet little thing in a princess gown, buckled snugly at five-points in her car seat, singing about the yumminess of fruit salad.

Then I blinked, and... OMIGOD! WHERE DID THOSE COME FROM??!!

After I recovered from hysterical blindness, my little angel announced I needed to take her shopping.

For a bra.

"I need it for my dance recital Sunday," she said. "My costume has really thin straps so the teacher said I should get a strapless bra."

I knew bra shopping was one thing she has done before (and would rather do) with the adult women in her life.

Why me, Lord? Why now?

Process of elimination. My wife was on a business trip; my sister on vacation.

"Uhhh," I said wittily, "To Target."

I was surprised by the size of Target's lingerie department. It's big. By big, I mean, Target's key demographic must be body doubles for Sofia Vergara. It was also dazzlingly colorful like one of those candy stores where the walls are lined with tube after tube of exotically flavored jellybeans.

After wandering around, we found the juniors section.

Seamless bandeau, structured bandeau, Spandau Ballet.

Scoop, demi, Ashton.

I had not been this overwhelmed by selections since I shopped Home Depot for sheet metal screws.

"Will this work?" I asked. "The tag says it's a convertible bra."

"No. It has straps."

"Doesn't convertible mean the top comes off?"

"I don't know," she says.

And I think to myself, I hope you never will until you're married.

Then I spotted a woman by the sports bras with a cart. Her cart was overflowing with a mish-mash of clothing, sporting goods and toys. More importantly, she wore a bright red jacket and a bull's eye name tag.

"Let me go ask that clerk..."

"Daddy, noooooooooooooooooooo!"

"All right," I sighed. "Just remember that answer when you're on stage and the girls make an unexpected curtain call."

Finally, we found some strapless bras. They were in hot pink. In "passion purple". Day Glo green. Vegas showgirls wear less flashy double-barreled catapults.

Eventually, we located a couple that would not be noticeable from a nautical mile in London fog. They also happened to be in her size.

Not that my daughter knew her bra size. That would have been too easy. I've been down this road before. Not with bras, but nearly every other piece of clothing my children own because in our house, this dad does most of the shopping from groceries to garage doors. Before we left the house, I went to my daughter's room, found one of her bras and checked the tag. The next time some marketing genius tells you women make the vast majority of family purchasing decisions in the United States, you have the permission of this member of the minority to kick that person squarely in the statisticals.

She headed to the fitting rooms, and I was alone.

I forgot what to do with my arms. Fold them? No. Hands in pockets? No -- NO!

This kept me perplexed while I waited. And waited...

Suddenly, I was a child again. Waist-high to a headless mannequin in a tube top and bell bottoms in some long-demolished women's department store. I'm confused. Lost. My mom has dragged me shopping with her again. The hopelessness. The suffering. The boredom... The boredom.

Things start pulling away and I'm falling down a hole walled with endless racks of frilly rack holders. I'm weightless. I'm floating! Below, I could almost see my boyish self...

Wait a sec.

I really could see my boyish self.

It was my nine-year-old son. I forgot we took him along on this expedition.

"Son," I said, extending my right arm and index finger.

"Pet supplies, office supplies, greeting cards. Choose your pleasure."

After a contemplative look, he picked greeting cards. I told him we'd be there in a few minutes.

The next morning, the sun still rose in the east.

And on Sunday, when my daughter bounded across the stage for her final curtsy, I was there applauding and standing proud and firm.

Just like her bosom.

WHATEVER SHE NEEDS ME TO BE

David Fetters, Columbus, OH

I know it sounds a little clichéd, but the second she grabbed my hand in the delivery room, I knew my daughter had me wrapped around her little finger. I knew I would do anything for her. It was the happiest moment of my life. I began dreaming of all the things I would teach her, not knowing at the time just how much she would teach me.

Since I was the parent at the lower paying job and my work had more flexibility, I pursued and obtained a new part-time position so I could care for her and we could avoid daycare costs. Being a stay-at-home dad/part-time employee was not a path any of the men in my family had ever followed. It didn't matter to me. I was not going to let stereotypical gender roles determine how I would raise my child. I was thrilled with having a daughter and I had no plans to let other people stop her from pursuing her own dreams no matter what they might turn out to be. It didn't take long in her life before I needed to step up to that challenge.

When my daughter was four-years-old, she wanted to be a firefighter for Halloween. Not a traditional little girl's choice, however, my wife and I were fine with it. She was excited, especially since she was going to a holiday party at her grandparent's church.

At one of the craft stations, we came across two little boys dressed up in Lycra superhero outfits. As soon as they saw her costume, they started making fun of her; telling her that because she was a girl, she couldn't be a firefighter. When I saw tears shimmering in her big brown eyes, I knew I needed to respond quickly. Realizing I was dealing with five-year-old boys in a patriarchal church where I was not a member, I also knew I needed to temper my response. Their parents, who said nothing to their children, simply smiled. I looked at the parents, then down at the boys. I explained to them she could be a firefighter just like they could be ballet dancers. The parents glared at me and I simply smiled back. My daughter laughed.

When she slipped her hand into mine as we went back to the party, I like to think she squeezed me just a little tighter.

Later, when my daughter was in first grade, she decided she wanted to join the Girl Scouts. However, when she tried to join the troop, we were told the ratio of adults to children in the troop was already at the maximum permitted level. One of her parents would have to volunteer to be a co-leader of the troop if she wanted to join. Since my wife had no desire to take on that role, the task fell to me. My personal scouting experience consisted of a torturous six weeks as a Boy Scout when I was twelve-years-old, but for my daughter, I looked into becoming an adult volunteer. Aware of how men in child care environments can be perceived, I gladly gave the Girl Scouts whatever they requested from me: background check, blood and hair samples, drug testing, etc. I even made sure the three references I provided were all non-related women. I was approved and my daughter was allowed to join. At scouting events, I was usually the only male in the room. Whenever I received a sexist remark suggesting I shouldn't be a Girl Scout Leader, I simply told them I had been in Girl Scouts longer than I was in Boy Scouts.

Once, I had to give a presentation in front of the entire Council. I was the only dad in the room and, somehow, my daughter sensed my apprehension. She grabbed my hand and gave me a kiss. I'm not sure I've ever been more proud.

My role as a Girl Scout leader and stay-at-home dad hasn't been the easiest thing in the world, but my daughter and the other girls in the troop accept me as their Cookie Dad. Together, we are learning you can break through the glass ceiling one fire helmet and one box of cookies at a time. While I know, eventually, she'll have to fight these battles on her own, I think she knows I'll always be there to slip my hand into hers and be whatever she needs me to be.

APP TO TRAVEL

Steven Grams, La Vista, NE

Conversations with four-year-olds are usually pretty entertaining. They can range from "I saw a train go down our street" to "Let's go to Lightning McQueen's house." As a dad, I am trained myself to never be caught off guard.

"I went to China this weekend," I heard from the back seat one morning from my talkative four-year old.

"Really, who'd you go with?" I asked, holding back a smile realizing she had a pretty serious look on her face.

"Myself! We had mac and cheese on the plane."

Interesting, as she had still yet to experience air travel, but now I really wanted to see where her imagination was going.

"What did you do sweetheart?" I asked through the rear view mirror.

"Oh, I went and saw Panda Bears and ate Chinese food and then I went on a train and went to France."

WOW! So China and France all in a weekend. Sounded busy to me. By train no less and she still made it back for pre-school on Monday. She told me about Paris in great detail, riding the metro, riding to the top of the Eiffel Tower, etc.

As she described her journey I believed, in my infinite wisdom, I was an awesome dad. I read a good selection of books to her on faraway places, watched travel shows with her, and always talked about the world and different places. I must have had her brain firing on all cylinders and now had her imagining travel.

"World's Best Dad" I believe the t-shirt reads.

She'll mention me when she's sworn in as the U.S. Secretary of State for filling her mind with the idea that our own backyard is not the only backyard in the world, I thought to myself. My place as the primary book reader, dinner cook, and general imagination-giver was going to pay off with reservations to any restaurant in the world!

When my wife came home that evening, I told her of all the wonderful things our daughter had said to me. I puffed up my chest and assumed the position on the pedestal for my gold medal. Then the crash occurred.

"I loaded a kid's world travel App on the iPad for her," she said. "She's already visited more countries than you and I combined."

Deflated, I shrunk back down to regular dad status. Defeated by the App Store. In a few days she had traveled the world in her mind. My efforts over the years resulted in more of an interest for Fancy Nancy, but no weekend trips to faraway places.

When little heads hit their pillows for the evening, I had some more time to talk to my always better half. I expressed my dismay that the iPad will get mentioned at her swearing in and confirmation hearing before Congress, and dear old dad will only be the one who helped pay for college.

After a few eye rolls, my wife went on to explain the whole story. The App was picked because of what I had read and done for her. She actually asked for a game with the Eiffel Tower, Leaning Tower of Pisa, and other places daddy showed pictures of and read about.

Take that Apple!

In our digital age, the tools available to us are incredible. The ability to get instant information on the road about where to eat, sleep, stop, and see the sights in real time is allowing more and more people to step out of their skin and not only travel, but travel independently. It allows us to show our kids, in an interactive setting, what the world looks like outside of their small world.

For our kids, books help open the door to finding and discovering a whole new world. Reading a book, looking at pictures, or just listening to a story makes the synapses in their brain fire. I love letting my kids use the iPad in the way they use it. I also love the fact that my little traveler can't wait to get out and see what her daddy has taught her. But to engage kids, and yourself in travel, reading a book paints a fascinating picture that keeps you wanting more. The beauty of the book is it gives kids a real desire to go to the place and see it for themselves instead of watching a video and being done with it.

I feel confident my night job of reading is still safe.

And so are my reservations.

OUR HOUSE RESTAURANT

Chris Routly, Portland, OR

All morning, the boys and I were out running various errands. When the boys figured out we were on our way home for lunch, they began to plead and whine, begging to go out for lunch instead. Their whining was par for the course and making my head hurt.

Honestly, lunch out sounded great to me. I don't mind not having to cook anything or clean up the inevitable mess! However, we had already eaten out that week and I wanted to honor the family budget. I had to put my foot down and say "no."

The whining escalated. The pain in my head neared an explosion.

"But Dadaaaaa, I really like going to restaurants…"

"Yeah, I wan go westawant tooooo…"

Suddenly an idea hit me. It might create a little bit more work for me, but if I pulled it off…

"Okay boys, listen up," I said. Miraculously, they did. "We're going to go to a restaurant. It's called *Our House*."

"*Our House Restaurant*?" asked Tucker, my five-year-old.

"That's right," I said. "*Our House Restaurant*. I think you'll really like it. The whole place is set up to look exactly like our house."

The boys giggled. I had them hooked. At the very least, the whining had stopped. The throbbing in my head abated.

When we arrived at Our House Restaurant, I jumped into the first of my many roles as "owner."

"*Our House Restaurant* wants you to feel right at home," I explained in my most dashing voice. "Please remove your shoes and put them by the door. Your hats and coats can be hung in the closet." They played along beautifully. "Now, if you will follow me, I will show you to your table. This way, please…"

"This looks just like our house!" observed Tucker.

"Yes, our design team is very thorough. See, we even replicated the toys scattered throughout the living room." I sat them down at our kitchen table in their usual seats and brought them each their Monkey and Bumble Bee water bottles. "Now if you'll excuse me, your server will be right with you."

I grabbed my colored markers and a piece of heavy photo paper. Quickly, I sketched out an illustrated menu for *Our House Restaurant*. I had no desire to turn myself into a short-order cook for my kids, so I kept the options very basic and limited to things I could fix in a hurry. They got two choices: a cheese quesadilla or a PB&J sandwich, and for sides, they could have apple slices and/or cucumbers.

Returning to the table with menu in hand, I took on the role of their server. I called them each "sir" as I presented them their options, from which they both selected PB&J with apple slices.

"Very good, sirs. I will pass on your order to the chef and, while you wait, here is an appetizer for you to enjoy," I said, laying down a small bowl of pita chips in front of each of them.

While I threw together their PB&Js and apples, they quietly munched on the pita chips. When I brought them their lunch, they ate it all, not fighting, or throwing food, or whining, or climbing onto the table. I was actually able to go sit in the living room and enjoy a cup of coffee, undisturbed. I couldn't remember the last time they both ate at home so well-behaved.

After their plates were clean, I returned to the table and asked if they had saved room for dessert. Well, OF COURSE they had, so I retrieved the basket of leftover Halloween candy from its hiding place and let them each select a treat. Again, they enjoyed them quietly. When they were all done, they left the table and went to play together for a bit before my three-year-old Coltrane needed his nap.

They didn't leave a tip, but I didn't complain.

Parenting is often all about figuring out what works for you and your kids on any given day. You have to try all sorts of things. You win some. You lose some. On this day, I went out on a limb, created some fun, had some fun myself, and somehow managed to have the smoothest lunchtime I could remember. This one goes in the "win" column.

I think *Our House Restaurant* might be expanding its hours to serve breakfast and dinner too. Maybe it's time to set up a Yelp page...

WHERE DID I COME FROM?

Stephen Kane, Bronxville, NY

"Oh, give me a break..." My son says in a low, nervous voice to himself. Mumbling and giggling are heard as the video being played on the big screen contains a cartoon image of a preteen girl becoming a young woman. My son tilts his head into my shoulder as the same video is now presenting a boy growing (all over I might add) through his teen years. The kids break out into an unsettling laughter as the screen is filled with tales of pubic hair, sweat glands, and reproductive organs. It's a bonding moment for fathers and their sons as we witness "Changing Bodies", a film providing helpful, accurate, age-appropriate information regarding the physical and psychological changes of puberty.

Two days before this night, the parents were invited to preview the short film, in a way, to pre-shock the parents into realizing that sooner or later someone is going to have to tell our kids where they came from. The health teacher conducting the lecture was straightforward and direct while talking about the sensitivities of the subject. The format was to be fathers and sons watching in one room and mothers and daughters in another. Parents were to sit with their kids; no huddles of kids on one side and parents in the back glued to their phones. "This is an important opportunity for the kids to foster and encourage comfortable and open communication between themselves and their parents," the teacher explained.

My pre-teen years never included a discussion regarding the "facts of life" let alone my changing body. How would I react to questions? How would I react if there were no questions? How would my son react to the answers?

Walking from our apartment to the school with my son, we discuss the evening's purpose and what to expect in the movie. We sit in the fourth row towards the center aisle for optimal viewing. The teacher introduces himself, outlines the evening's agenda and proceeds to pass around a handout containing about thirty-four questions, each containing a True, False, or Not Sure answer. My son glances at the questionnaire and, as I watch his eyes move down the page, he giggles, then eyebrow scrunches concluding with some jaw-dropping reactions. The teacher reads each question and the boys respond out loud. I scan the room to see the other dads' reactions. Again, exhibits of smiles, squirms, and the popular jaw-dropping pose.

Here is a sample of some of the True/False/Not Sure questions:

• If a boy has pimples during puberty, he will probably have them all his life.

• Most boys stop growing at the age of fourteen ("I hope not!" someone screams).

• Penis size has nothing to do with height, muscle build, or sexual abilities.

• Wet dreams are common for most boys. (This is where my son turns to me and asks, "Did I have any yet?")

• Erections can occur for no apparent reason at all. (Gasp from the crowd.)

• Voice changes are caused by the growth of the larynx or voice box. (A boy asks if there is also a laugh box.)

• Most women have a period every 28 days.

• Boys should pay extra attention to their nutritional balance when they enter puberty.

Now we are set to watch the movie. The movie covers the body changes in girls as well as boys in an effort to teach respect and privacy. "After all," the teacher explains, "there will be moments for boys and for girls to be in situations where discretion is needed." Then the teacher asks, "What would be an awkward time for a boy to get an erection?" A boy in the front row blurts out, "Right now?" The ensuing laughter eases the uneasiness in the room. The movie concludes with children on a field trip, feeling happy and content, while our kids are fidgety and tense.

The teacher turns off the projector and approaches a few more topics with both kids and parents participating in the discussion, allowing the apprehension to subside. By the end of the evening, everyone is relaxed and feeling positive when the teacher recalls the time his oldest of three daughters asked him: "Where did I come from?" After gingerly detailing the attributes of men and women, the genetics of reproduction and scientifically laying out the steps to how babies are made, his daughter interrupts him and shrieks, "Geez dad! I just wanted to know what hospital I was born in!"

Sometimes, the teacher reminds us, the simplest answers are the best ones.

NOT AFRAID OF A QUESTION MARK, OR A PERIOD

Mike Sager, Lee's Summit, MO

nswering my daughter's many questions was not always easy. The more I did it, though, the easier it was. One day, she would have questions about gravity and the next day, she would ask about the difference between girls and boys. I made sure I was able to answer each and every question with equal enthusiasm. I never said, "Go ask your mother." As the primary custodial parent, I sucked it up and made sure she knew I was the go-to-guy for anything she needed.

At age eight, when she developed breast buds, she came to me very worried. I assured her that even though it was a bit painful, it was perfectly natural. With her sitting beside me, I pulled up a couple of websites. I pointed out how many references there were for "painful knots under my nipples." It was reassuring to her. This was not a disaster. This was perfectly natural. I explained to her this was the beginning of puberty. I described all the things that were going to happen over the next few years. I reassured her I would answer any question; all she needed to do was ask.

I knew this day would come. I told myself I was ready. There would be lots of questions over the next few years and I remembered how scary it had been for me.

A couple weeks later, she complained about a stomach ache. I went over the pain with her. Was it a sharp stabbing pain? Does it last a long time, or come then go away? Was it a throbbing pain that persists in the same spot? It could be anything from something she ate to a pulled muscle. Of course, it could also have been puberty. I could have easily blown it off and waited to see if it went away, but what if it was cramps? Just to be sure, we talked about puberty again. I described all the things that would happen over the next few years. I suggested this could be, but might not be, related to her period and we would watch and see if it lasted. I went over what to do if her period happened while she was at school. I assured her it happened to every girl and the school nurse would know what to do. I was seriously hoping this was not the issue, but I wanted her to be prepared.

There were no more sharp pains over the next few months and I breathed a sigh of relief. I asked her about it every once in a while. I did not make a big deal, just inquired. She was good with it.

About six months later, I got a call to her bedroom. Her underwear was halfway down and she was pointing to a spot on her underwear. It was small, about the size of a dime. But it was undeniable what it was.

"What is that, Dad?"

Without hesitation, I sat beside her and gave her a big hug. "My little girl is becoming a young woman!" I said. She was smiling but still needed some more verification. "That is your first period," I explained.

I went to the hall closet and came back with a pad. I then proceeded to demonstrate how to put it in her underwear. When I had the pad secured, I held open the underwear as if she would step into them, the way we had done thousands of times before.

She looked at me and said, "I can put on my own underwear, Dad."

"Of course you can," I said. She took them from me and climbed in on her own. I could not remember the last time I helped her put on her clothes, but it seemed like yesterday.

I showed her how small the package for the pad was, how easily she could carry it in a pocket of her backpack, perfect for "just in case" moments. We went over the importance of changing them regularly and marking the date on a calendar. She went over to the calendar on her wall. I was starting to say how we could make a code so we could track her periods, maybe a different color pen or a different symbol. I was trying to emphasize the importance of keeping track without embarrassing her. She already had it figured out. She put a big red "P" with a circle around it.

Then I said, "Or we could just use a big red 'P' on the calendar. That works too."

I hugged her again and said, "I think we should go out and celebrate. Do you want to get some ice cream after dance practice?" She was all smiles now and enthusiastic for the celebration.

"Mom is going to be so surprised when she finds out," she said. "She is going to, like, see my underwear on the floor with a pad in it and be like, 'My little girl is grown up!'"

And there it was, the culmination of my efforts. Most of a decade spent as the primary caregiver, mentor, and confidant. I had worried about this moment, I had dreaded this moment, but I had also looked forward to it, and planned for it.

Not only did she come to me at this special moment, but evidently her mother was not even going to know about it until she found out by accident. I was proud that I, her dad, was her secret feminine confidante.

"Two more things," I added. "First, why don't we call your mom and tell her the big news? Then we can discuss the proper way to dispose of pads so they never, ever, under any circumstances, show up on the floor."

PART FIVE

DAD'S WAY: DIFFERENT, NOT WRONG

"We were exploring the local forest. I was encouraging my son to climb a tree or a mud bank or walk along a wall and jump off the end. My wife kept telling him to get down. She would like to wrap him up in cotton wool. I want him to learn and explore and bumps and bruises are part of life."
- *Nathan Fussell, father of two in Aberdaugleddau, Pembrokeshire, United Kingdom*

NAILING FATHERHOOD

Shannon Carpenter, Lee's Summit, MO

I want my daughter to grow up confident, sure of herself. I want her to be able to rely on herself; to believe if something needs to be done, she is the one to do it. I want her to be assertive, to set goals and attain them. I want her to grab her victories, learn from her losses and plan for the future.

So I gave her my nail gun.

Hear me out; this is genius.

I build furniture on occasion. A chair here, an outdoor table there. I get immense satisfaction from it. I look at a completed project and think to myself, yup, I would totally have sex with me. I am confident, even when I mess up. I am confident I can identify the mistake, the actions leading to the mistake, and the necessary steps to correct that mistake.

Or glue. I can always use more glue.

This is what I want for my daughter and there is no better time to start this than when she is five. We bought an old antique bed from a garage sale, five bucks. It appears I am cheap. But when others looked at the 60-year-old bed and saw a cracked headboard and two busted legs, I saw greatness and opportunity. I saw a chance to work with my daughter; to begin to teach her the lessons I thought she would need as a woman.

We took the bed home in pieces and set it up in my garage. We took off the busted legs. We pried off the old molding on the headboard and then had a quick sword fight with it because, let's face it, sword fights are always cool.

We chose poplar for the leg replacements because my daughter liked the green swirls. Good enough for me. I planed them and joined them, letting her do the glue work. If you can glue paper, you can glue wood. She took the project seriously for a five-year-old; I was quite proud. We shaped the legs on the table saw and touched them up with the router. Repeat. And bam: two new legs.

The headboard was a bit trickier but that's okay. If there isn't a challenge to a build, why build at all? Over a very nice game of Candyland, we decided it wouldn't be too hard to glue the headboard back together if we used some straps instead of straight clamps. My daughter ran and got "daddy's special ropes" and boom! More glue work and 24 hours later, our headboard was back in one piece.

Now the only thing left was nailing on the molding. I cranked up the air compressor, put eye goggles and ear protectors on my daughter and me and brought our wood over to the headboard.

This was by far the coolest thing she had ever done in her entire life, ever, ever. I know this because she told me. I took her to Disney World but I didn't bring that up because, honestly, this was pretty cool. Completing a project with your kid is a special kind of cool; one that will last with me a lot longer than Mickey. No offense Mr. Mouse.

I tutored my daughter about the safety rules of handing a nail gun. Then I held the molding up and guided her hand. She placed the gun where she wanted the nail to go, took a big breath, squinted one eye behind her goggles, and bam, pulled the trigger. She squealed in delight. I had to remind her that we don't jump up and down with a nail gun in hand. We quickly finished the rest of the molding, put the bed back together and put on the new legs. I was proud of my little girl and she was proud of herself. We called mom and sent her pictures of all the things she had done because she is a big girl now, she can do it.

That was the confidence I was looking for; that right there.

"What color do you want to paint your new bed, honey?" I asked her.

"PURPLE! PURPLE! PURPLE! PURPLE!" she said.

"Cool, I dig purple. But how about we just do the inside purple?"

SINK OR SWIM

Jason Ward, Benbrook, TX

Let me set the scene. It's a wintry, cold February afternoon. My then five-year-old son and I are trying to make the most of a short-lived sunny day. He is playing on the concrete decking around our backyard pool and I'm focused on my weekend honey-dos. I have no desire to take the Polar Bear Plunge, so I'm being very cautious with my steps as I fish the fallen red oak leaves from the icy-cold water. My son, like most young boys, is not so careful. My wife and I never leave him unattended or unsupervised around the pool, but it only took three seconds. One-one thousand (silence)... two-one thousand (splash)... three-one thousand (silence). He apparently reached for something in the pool which was all it took for him to tumble into the deep end.

I am no more than four yards away and our son is already a great swimmer, but the shock of the 42-degree water was enough that it must have knocked the air right out of his lungs as soon as he hit the surface. Without air, he sank to a depth of about six feet almost instantly. On a normal day, my protective fatherly instinct would have inspired me to dive in fully clothed... wallet, cell phone and all... but today my own survival instincts made me hesitate to jump into the cold, cold water. Instead, I looked down into the blue abyss and saw on his way to the bottom, he was staring straight up at me with panic on his face. His wide blue eyes told me he was looking to me to do something about this frightening predicament.

I know my son. I know his capabilities. We taught him how to hold his breath under water when he was less than a year old. We taught him to swim when he was three-years-old, and by his fourth summer, he was routinely diving eight feet below the surface to fetch "treasures" from the bottom. He is not afraid of the water.

So, rather than be his rescuer, I made a different decision. He looked at my eyes and I looked at his. I made the same paddling hand motions I had made to him many times before while teaching him to swim. He understood. He kicked his little legs and brought himself to the surface to grab my outstretched hand. I pulled him out expecting him to immediately cry out of fear or panic, but he didn't. Instead of fear, what I saw in his eyes was confidence. Despite his immediate need to have his daddy save him from a dangerous and scary situation, he overcame his fear and fought his way to the surface.

I admit that I really did not want to jump into the cold water. I also admit part of me really wanted to be his hero. But since that day, I've often thought about this as an analogy to parenthood. We are often faced with a tough decision… do we pull them out when they fall into the deep end? Or do we encourage them to swim to the top on their own?

Every day as fathers, we have the opportunity to help our children learn the skills and life lessons they will need someday when they are in a tough situation. If we are not careful, we can allow ourselves as parents to become overly relied upon life vests. Our children grow accustomed to reaching for us rather than relying on their own instincts. Someday, they may reach for a life vest that is not there. Then what's it going to be? Sink or swim?

CARTOONS AND WATERMELONS

John Elous, Chicago, IL

I have an acute sense of how little time I spend with my ten-year-old daughter, and I have come to the realization over the last two or three years how much of her life I am missing.

I live in Downtown Chicago and commute 45 minutes to my office in the suburbs. I leave the house well before my daughter wakes up; sometimes it feels like the middle of the night, to get a run in before work, and to beat some of the traffic. Every 15 minute delay adds 20 minutes to the commute as you get closer to "rush hour" which, for anyone who knows Chicago, starts at 6:00 a.m. and ends at 7:00 p.m.

The truth is, staying ahead (or behind the traffic in the evening) is only partially the motivator for arriving early or leaving the office late. I get there early to simply keep my head above water. I use the hour before the majority of my co-workers arrive to prepare for my usual routine of business reviews, ad hoc meetings and steady stream of email. During the week, I struggle to leave the office by 6:30 p.m., which means I usually get home around 8:00 p.m., which is bedtime for my daughter.

I love my work. My wife would say I have an unhealthy level of passion for it. She is extremely supportive, though, and kindly feigns interest when I feel compelled to tell her about some work-related event or business success. I really should dial it back. I know this to be true when my daughter jumps into a conversation between my wife and I and offers advice on some business deal, or work dilemma.

Clearly my daughter misses me. I miss her too. For the past several years, I have done two things on a consistent basis to help make up for our lack of time together. I may not be around when she wakes up, nor do I often get home before she goes to bed at night, but I take great pleasure in knowing she is thinking of me. To help remind her of me during the day, I fell in the habit of making little cartoons for her lunch box. They started out as little jokes, but quickly evolved to be full-blown animations. I am no artist; in fact the creative execution of my "Laugh out Loud Lunches" is not going to be making *The New Yorker* any time soon.

Often, they are scribbled on a scrap of paper while lying in bed at night, or standing at the kitchen counter drinking a cup of coffee before I leave the house in the morning. I dream these things up while sitting in traffic, or occasionally, I shamelessly copy a joke I heard, or saw somewhere over the course of the day. My wife will fold them up and slip them into my daughter's lunch bag, long after I have left for the office. When I am not traveling, I am usually good for at least one or two a week.

Apparently my little cartoons are a hit in the school lunchroom. My daughter tells me they are passed around the lunch table for a group critique, and more times than not, the kids like them. The more esoteric cartoons are passed to the teacher for explanation and evaluation. My wife tells me she knows how well my "Laugh Out Loud Lunch" was received by my daughter and friends about five minutes into the car ride home. Strangely, getting a positive review is something I look forward to hearing. I love to think of her reading the cartoons and (hopefully) laughing and thinking about what a great guy her dad is.

The second outlet I use to compensate for my absence is watermelon sculpture. She loves watermelon, always has. When my wife was pregnant, she craved watermelon at all hours of the day and night. I'm not sure if there is any biological evidence to support why my daughter loves it so much, but she eats it almost every day. So, when I prepare breakfast on the weekends, there is inevitably watermelon on the plate. However, I don't just slice the melon, I sculpt! I will arrange the melon on a plate and, to great fanfare, present it to my bleary-eyed daughter. The highlight of my day is watching her face as she sees her breakfast and the figure I have carved.

As I am sitting on an airplane somewhere far away from my family, or sitting in my car during my commute to work, I often think of the look on her face in that instant. I have no idea what, if anything, she is thinking, but I like to think when she is an adult, she will look back on her childhood and remember these sculptures and drawings. My hope is she will recognize these little gestures as a symbol of my love for her, and even if dad was gone most of the week, he tried hard to stay connected.

WRESTLING WITH FATHERHOOD

Jason Greene, Astoria, NY

My son was lying on the couch and said those words all parents hate, "I'm bored." He writhed and complained for a while. The complaining crawled up my spine as I tried to work on a new play I had been writing. He wanted my attention. When I didn't want to give it, he lamented. Loudly.

My son is like so many other kids. He has too many toys, but there are times when no toy seems to fit the desired need. He wants to be entertained. He wants to be physical. He wants interaction with me.

Realizing I wasn't going to get any work done anyway, I closed the laptop and set it aside. I cleared a space on the floor, gave him a mean look and said, "Let's go!"

Those two words mean only one thing in our house — a wrestling match. My son loves to wrestle more than anything else. I knew it would make his day.

We squared off and circled one another. He went in for the shoot, grabbing my legs in an attempt to take me down, but not this time. I quickly hoisted his cinder block-styled body into the air and spun him around. After setting him down, I went for my favorite hold: the cross-face chicken wing. Long time pro-wrestling fans will be familiar with this hold because it was made famous by the legendary 70's superstar, Bob Backlund. I had my son on his back, but he fought through, spun around, sat on my chest, and began his version of ground and pound. He's allowed to hit me in the chest and stomach but not the face. And, before children's services pay me a visit, no child is harmed in our wrestling matches; only dads.

Our match went back and forth with both of us trying Mixed Martial Arts moves such as the Kimora, Rear Naked Choke, Omoplata, and Triangle Choke. We also used pro-wrestling moves such as The Sleeper,

Body Press, and my personal favorite, the Von Erich Iron Claw.

We sweated and tossed one another around. Occasionally, foreign objects in the form of pillows and stuffed animals were tossed into the ring (I bet the Hard-Core Wrestling Legend Mike Foley never thought of using The Dreaded Goose Down Feather Pillow Throw). As my body was telling me it was time to quit, I looked up at the clock and realized we had been wrestling for over an hour. We were both exhausted. I stood up and he once again shot for my legs. This time, I folded like a wet blanket and crumpled to the floor. He covered me and got the three count. Our Iron Man match had come to an end. His boredom was cured. We hugged and told each other, "I love you." He ran off to play with some toys, while I slumped against the couch. Hoisting him up in the air was much harder than it used to be.

Although my play-writing goal was not accomplished for the day, it was time well spent. He'll be nine in a couple of months and then soon, he'll be 18. I doubt he'll let me wrestle with him then. But, if I ever hear him say, "I'm bored," even when he's 18, I'll say, "Let's go!" Most likely he will roll his eyes then instead of joining me in the rink. I thought about that as he walked away and I smiled to myself.

From somewhere else in the house, I heard the running feet of my daughter. She burst into the living room and yelled, "Let's Go!" I pulled myself up, gave her a sneer and watched as she shot in for my legs. She failed to take me down, and I lifted her into the air.

Iron Man match number 2 was under way.

WHERE'S ALICE?

Mike Sager, Lee's Summit, MO

One night in the middle of winter, we had taken our bath, brushed our teeth, read a story, sang three songs, and were at the part of the evening where I turn out the light so my then five-year old daughter Claire can go to sleep. That is the moment when she asks, "Daddy, would you get Alice the Camel for me?" I sigh. Sometimes these little last minute requests are a precursor for a long evening of trying to get a little girl to go to sleep. It may lead to, "Can I have a drink of water?" "Can I sleep in your bed?" "Can I have something to eat?" "Is tomorrow going to be a snow day?" "Can I watch cartoons?" The list goes on. However, Alice the Camel is, after all, Alice the Camel. How sad it would be for a little girl to be crying in bed wondering where Alice is? And how sad would it be for Alice to be tucked away in a chair somewhere wondering where her little girl is? I am not sure which is worse.

"Where is Alice?" I ask as I walk out of her room. "By the computer," she gingerly answers. She does not start to get out of bed to help look. This is a good sign. If she starts to get out of bed, it means we have to hunt for more animals.

As I look around the office trying to find Alice, it occurs to me that I had not seen Alice in a couple days. The night before, Claire fell asleep in my arms in front of the TV. The night before, she fell asleep clutching Green Alligator. As I realize Alice is not in the office, I head toward the living room. After the kitchen, I headed to the bathroom, the master bedroom, the hallway, and another bathroom, before I find myself back in Claire's room looking under blankets and sheets.

"I just looked there, Daddy!" There is a touch of panic in her voice. It has been a while and she realizes I am about to stop looking. I reach for Ponca the Turtle. "Here, Ponca is feeling a little lonely right now. Why don't you sleep with Ponca?"

The look on her face tells me this might have worked had I tried it a few minutes ago, but the gig is up. She knows Alice is missing. "Where did you have her last?" I ask, knowing full well asking a five-year-old to remember where she set down her Camel is a little like asking her to do long division.

"I think we took her in the car!"

Alice does not normally get to leave the house so we can avoid situations like this. If we absolutely have to take someone, we usually take Marvin the Shark. He is well-traveled and has seen most of the U.S. from Miami to Seattle. He has, in fact, wandered off a few times, but has always managed to find his way back home. He can be trusted past the door. But Alice is a kinder, gentler animal and would not feel comfortable wandering around in the big world. Perhaps she spent too much time tucked under the arm of a little girl to get a good enough taste of independence to cope with open spaces.

I thought back and could not remember taking Alice out of the house. Claire seemed convinced. Two days before, we had wandered home late in the afternoon and I had carried her sleeping body into the house. Was Alice with her then? Did Alice drop in the yard on the way in? None of these options showed much hope but I went to the door and put on my boots.

Outside, the snow in the yard was in big clumpy piles where we had played pretty hard when the snow first came down. Two snowmen were still standing guard in front of the house. I ventured into the wind and falling snow to check the car. No luck. As I headed back to the house, I kicked all the piles of snow that could have hidden the body of a small stuffed camel covered by the never-ending snowfall that had graced us that week. Every kick caught my breath a little. I was not excited about finding a wet, frozen camel, though I suppose it would have been a good thing to finally know Alice's fate.

I looked up and could see Claire's silhouette through the window as she followed me with her eyes in my search. I imagined the tears welled up in her eyes as she saw me heading toward the door empty-handed.

As I entered, she was quick to ask, "Did you find Alice?" Tears were all the way down her cheeks. She already knew the answer. "Why don't we go to bed honey? We will find Alice tomorrow." Unfortunately, this was never going to be a satisfactory answer but I carried her up the stairs and laid her in bed. I kissed her on the cheek and assured her we would find Alice the Camel in the morning. She was crying as I walked out the door.

I resumed the search. Entering my room, I remembered Claire crawling into bed with me the morning before last. Maybe Alice had come with her. I washed the sheets that day but did not remember finding a camel in the bed. Then it occurred to me there was only one room in the house I did not check. Had Alice been hidden in the sheets when I put them in the laundry? I went into the garage. As I started for the washer, there was Alice on the floor. I picked her up. She was dry. She did not smell freshly washed or dried. I suspect Alice, realizing she was about to go in the wash, had avoided the disaster by squirming out of the sheets and settling on the floor. Camels do not seem to appreciate baths any more than little girls. It was a close call.

I carried Alice back upstairs, silently scolding her for causing such a panic. Alice seemed altogether delighted to be out of the cold garage and off the floor and pretty much ignored me.

Claire stopped sniffling as I entered her room. As I parted the princess curtain hanging over her bed to hand her Alice the Camel, she was already reaching for her. She tucked Alice under her arm. I sat there for a few minutes stroking her hair as the last of her sniffles went away and she and Alice drifted off to sleep.

LITTLE WHITE LIE

Eric Jefferson, Chicago, IL

"Jayla lied to me tonight," I thought while looking out over the alley from the back porch in the cool Chicago night. I was trying not to place too much importance on the event but simultaneously felt like we had reached the end of an era. An end to the days when I could believe whatever this little one told me, at least after a few well-placed questions.

Her untruths to this point, as a four-year-old, had consisted only of miscommunication and the occasional feeble attempt to blame a mistake on an imaginary friend. These stories always self-imploded with the simple suggestion they might not be true. Not this time. This time, it was a bald face lie. It didn't run from my interrogation like fleeting shadows when the curtains are flung open. This one stood its ground and looked at me through the big blue eyes of my sweet little girl.

"I'm going to ask you again," I started. "Did you try to feed Bobo tonight without asking me?"

I had already covered this ground three times and had been met with incredulity and faux injury. The sincerity of her claim to innocence was so genuine, on the face of it, I began searching for other explanations for the fish food pellets covering the water like so many berries in a Wisconsin cranberry marsh. Had I been over-feeding the fish for days and not realized it? No, there was only one explanation. Finally, I told Jayla I knew it was either she or her mother and I was going to call her mom to find out. One last time I tried, "Is there anything you need to tell me before I call your mom? You're going to be in bigger trouble if I have to make a call to find out you are lying to me." Her gaze shifted downward and her lips quivered momentarily.

That's when she came clean. "It was me, Daddy. I fed Bobo too much. I climbed up on the chair and put some food in the aquarium. I'm sorry. I just wanted to do it." I had to stiffen my upper lip. I let out a sigh of relief

145

that she hadn't held on to the fib any longer.

Unfortunately, Bobo had been sickly for days and this was probably going to be the straw that broke the fish's back, as it were. More importantly, messing with the aquarium had been addressed before. She knew it was against the rules.

She took her lumps. I had a long talk with her, reminding her to look in my eyes while I was talking; a trick I learned from many a lecture in the penetrating gaze of my father's eyes. She accepted there would be no TV this weekend and would have an early bedtime. She came to terms with my disappointment.

Later that evening, I could see Bobo was far too stoic. He had flared his fins at the passing giants for the last time. Jayla could see as well as I; he was not going to make it. I knew the line of Bobo was over; I had replaced other deceased Betta without her knowledge before, but not this time. I knew what would come next.

"Daddy, I'm sorry I made Bobo dead!" she whimpered and followed with sobs. I delivered a swift hug and took some care in explaining to her Bobo had been sick for days. I told her while over-feeding a fish can make them sick, I had found the problem in time. He died, I assured her, of his pre-existing condition and possibly from my less than expert fish-handling. Just like that, the prosecutor became the perjurer. My motives were different, but the act the same.

Later, as I stood on the porch, the cold started to bite so I ended my reflection and stepped inside. I knew we would buy another fish in the morning if the store was open. It would be Easter morning, but there would be no resurrection for Bobo this time. Another of childhood's fantasies would be dispelled. Pets don't live forever. A lesson was learned and I grudgingly accepted another unwelcome step in the march toward my daughter's maturity.

Easter morning, Jayla and I buried Bobo. I reminded her Bobo was loved and cared for all the days of his life and how he would now return to the Earth to support the growth of other living things.

"Like trees and butterflies?" she asked with a little smile. "Yes, kiddo, just like that. Trees and butterflies."

At the pet store, Jayla inspected the colorful inhabitants of the tanks. Eventually, we walked away with a new red Betta which Jayla named "John".

Welcome to our home, John. Don't be afraid of the giants. You will be safe, fed regularly, and will see a lot of interesting life zipping by in the curvature of your tank if you stick around. If, however, you do decide to go quietly into the night… try to do so when Jayla isn't looking, okay? She's had enough lessons in death for a while so, if you kick the bucket, I'll track down your twin and replace you before you can say "little white lie."

THE FIGHT

Al Watts, South Elgin, IL

The cul-de-sac was filled with bikes, balls and Barbies; in other words, a typical sunny afternoon.

The kids in the cul-de-sac - so many you couldn't count them - were going from one toy to the next like cats on caffeine. If your garage is open on the cul-de-sac, or "the circle" as the kids called it, your toys are available to anyone to play with. It is a little like socialism.

I was seated on my nylon folding chair throne in the shadow of our garage, a book in my hand with hopes of opening it. This was always a dream unrealized as I was a father of three children under the age of six at the time. Instead of my eyes gliding along the pages of my novel, I had them focused on my kids and their many neighborhood friends making sure they were safe.

Our nearly four-year-old daughter, Macy, had recently received a new bike. It was a pink Barbie bike with gleaming white training wheels and a silver bell; the coveted item on the circle. All the kids wanted a turn riding the newest item and none of them were getting one. Macy proudly rode her new bike around and around the circle. All her friends were envious and she knew it.

For a brief moment, she became distracted. She saw a tricycle belonging to one of the neighbors she wanted to ride. She dismounted her bike at the end of our driveway and ran to the tricycle. That's where he saw the opportunity he had been waiting for.

Our neighbor's son was the same age as Macy and had been at the front of the begging line to ride the new bike. When Macy finally hopped off, he ran over and jumped on.

I sat up in my chair. I wondered if Macy would notice. If she did notice, I wondered what she would do. She, like most other three-year-olds, was not a fan of sharing.

As soon as she made it to the tricycle, she looked back to see her friend mounting her bike. Her brand new bike. She abandoned all thoughts of the tricycle, ran back across our driveway, and grabbed the handle bars of her bike before the neighbor boy could start pedaling.

The brawl was on.

He smacked her on top of her helmet. She smacked him back on the top of his helmet. I stood up, but stayed where I was. She needs to solve her own problems, I said to myself. Daddy will not always be there to save her.

WHACK! Again, she hit her friend on the helmet.

WHACK! He hit her back.

They both began screaming at each other. Tears were streaming down their cheeks.

WHACK! WHACK! WHACK! WHACK!

Back and forth, faster and faster, harder and harder, they slammed the helmet of their opponent. Neither would let go of the bike. Neither would give in.

Now my daughter started pulling on her bike. WHACK! WHACK! WHACK! Her friend hit her over the head. WHACK! She hit back while pulling the bike with her other hand. I stood still. I watched with anticipation. I knew they weren't hurting each other by hitting each other on their helmets, but I was ready to spring to action in case they started making body blows.

WHACK!

WHACK!

Then, with one more correctly timed WHACK! and a pull, my daughter freed her bike from the grip of her friend. To consummate her conquest, she immediately mounted her treasure and rode away to the howls of her friend standing at the end of our driveway, defeated and crying.

I casually walked over to him and gave him a little hug which he pushed away. I then grabbed a nearby tricycle and encouraged him to ride it. He ripped it out of my hand, sat down and rode away.

My daughter and this boy had no more disagreements after that. In fact, they became very good friends who rarely argued again.

I was proud of my daughter for asserting herself and not backing down, win or lose. I was proud of her for solving her own problem even though I would have preferred her to use her words instead of her hands. I was also proud of myself for not intervening. Part of being a dad is knowing when not to interfere.

The world beyond the circle is not always fair. I want my kids to always work with others to solve their problems. When push comes to shove, though, I don't want them to be knocked down. I want them to stand up for themselves. Too soon, I won't be standing 30 feet away ready to help. I know, no matter how hard it is, if I give them the opportunities to fail and succeed, they will be better prepared.

WHY?

Scotty Schrier, Riverview, FL

I have a weekly meet-up for dads every Monday evening. It's simply called "Dads Group". We sit around and swap stories from the trenches. The dads with toddlers cringe when the dads with teens start talking. The dads with teens nod knowingly when the toddler dads start talking. In sharing our horror stories, we bond. We soon learn we aren't the only ones struggling out there. It's nice being able to just unload or brag without feeling judged.

One week, we talked about how our kids seem to behave better away from home. During the conversations I noticed there was something being said by almost every dad, especially me:

"Why?"

One guy was telling a story about going on vacation. His young son, with no provocation or asking, opened his suitcase and unpacked all of his clothes and put them in the dresser drawers at the hotel. The dad was dumbfounded. He was in awe of what his son did. He was proud of him. (I know, because he beamed while telling the story.) Then he said it. "Son, why can't you do that at home?"

It made me think of the time I watched my son help clean up the nursery at our church one Sunday. He put the toys away and was a very big helper. Then I said it. "Why don't you do that at home?"

As parents, we all do it.

"Why did you do that?"

"Why are you crying?"

"Why won't you get dressed?"

Why... why... why...

Why, indeed? To what end? To get to the bottom of things, of course! But in doing so, I realized the why's are like toxic little pieces of candy. By asking "why?" I am slowly whittling away at my son. It dawned on me during the dad group conversation that asking: "Why don't you do that at home?" wasn't praising my son for the good job he did. It wasn't telling him how proud I was for being so responsible. I was telling him that he's normally wrong. In a very subtle way, I was telling him he's a screw-up.

The clouds opened and I saw something I hadn't seen before:

"Why?" is accusatory. "What?" is inquisitive.

Since then, I have tried to change my "Why?" to "What?" It hasn't been easy.

"Why are you crying?" becomes "What's wrong?"

"Why won't you get dressed?" becomes "What would you rather be doing right now?"

Instead of looking for one-word answers, which are usually "Dunno," I'm opening a channel of dialogue. My son is more likely to tell me what's wrong with him if I ask him what's wrong. Asking "What?" gives him an implied hope I can help make things better. When he tells me what he'd rather be doing instead of getting dressed, I can then explain he needs to get dressed to do the thing he really wants to do.

This change in my behavior give me an opportunity to listen more to my son.

Being a dad is not always easy. I lapse on occasion. But one day, I hope to have the whys down to a minimum.

What's my reasoning for this? I want to pave the road to open communications now, when he's a toddler. I don't want to try to convince him as a teenager I'm ready to hear him out. If I don't listen to him now, he won't believe I will by then. So, I'm paying it forward. I hope it works and when Future Me reads this, he buys me a beer.

I'm sure he will. Future Me is a pretty radical dude.

Sorry, Past Me just sneaked that in.

GO WITH THE FLOW

Annette Acosta-Dickson, MD, Kansas City, MO

There was a time when I had it all.

My husband Brian, who had relapsed leukemia after two years of chemotherapy, was recovering slowly but steadily from a stem cell transplant. Our daughter's conception while he was still on chemotherapy was a miracle to both of us. I graduated from residency, had her shortly afterwards, and started my new job when she was only eight weeks old. We had no family nearby, but a steady stream of relatives from both sides visited frequently and helped us through a rough transition year.

I envied my husband staying home with our daughter every day while I went to work. When he was strong enough and the last of our family help flew the coop, we decided this arrangement worked for us. Raising her was the most important task we had.

I watched both of them blossom: my husband into a more patient version of himself, kind but firm. When we were new parents meeting others for the first time and they asked what he did, my husband would reply "Unix administrator" which was his last job before the relapse and stem cell transplant caused an abrupt change in our plans. After he and our daughter became regulars in the local at-home dads playgroup, Brian replied to the same question with pride, some chest-puffing, and a twinkle in his eye, that he was an at-home dad.

Conventional wisdom says we usually don't appreciate what we have while we have it. When I was diagnosed with breast cancer and had to endure chemotherapy - which didn't measure up to a fifth of what Brian had endured - Brian knew, without asking, how I felt and what I was thinking. He used to describe going through his stem cell transplant as fighting a gigantic man-eating monster, being eaten up alive, chewed up, and spit back out again. It sounds cliché, but my comparably pale experience allowed me to truly appreciate the difficulty of what he had been through.

Brian also had the endurance of a saint, and complained little about the side-effects of his treatments. One of the long-term effects of high-dose steroids received before his first transplant was avascular necrosis of the hips: the normal ball shape of his hip joints lost circulation and flattened making his hips literally square pegs in round sockets. He limped a little when walking, and winced if he had to clamber down to the floor to play with us, but otherwise grumbled very little.

When he relapsed again right before his 32nd birthday, he went back into the hospital with the same matter-of-fact approach he always did to treatment, as if to say, "Tell me what I have to do so I can get back to my life." Our daughter was three years old at the time and loved stuffed animals. Brian would use her stuffed animals as puppets and entertain her with voices that sounded like a cross between Donald Duck and Yoda. She and I wandered into a toy store one day and decided to pick up a stuffed version of Squirt, the kid turtle from *Finding Nemo*, for Brian's birthday so he would have "his squirt" with him even if they were separated while he was in the hospital.

Brian's parenting style was akin to Crush's, Squirt's dad. He was calm and generally laid back, in contrast to my Type A personality. I am convinced our daughter's nature, both gentle and adventurous, is a direct product of my husband's influence. She is turning out to be far better than if her neurotic, paranoid mother had been her early primary caregiver instead.

We went through a rough, scary patch of touch-and-go for two weeks, during which Brian drifted in and out of consciousness and we almost lost him. I knew he was back when his sense of humor returned. I came to visit after work one day and he was sitting up, almost as bright-eyed as normal. "Where's Squirt?" he asked.

"You don't remember?" He had, indeed, no memory of the lapsed time, which was just as well because it was horrible. Brian was in pain, angry and shouting. He had vomited all over Squirt on a particularly bad day, so Squirt had gone home to swim in several hot wash cycles. Our toddler found Squirt on the drying rack and decided Squirt belonged with her until Daddy needed him back. Squirt went back to the hospital to keep Brian company the rest of the week until he came home.

It took several months for everything to fall into place so Brian could receive a second stem cell transplant at MD Anderson. We sent our princess to my mother's for two months while I lived with Brian at the hospital. His parents took over for me after that so I could go back to work but it meant our daughter and I only saw him a couple of weekends that summer. Nine months later, when he had recovered some strength, we planned to take our princess to see the real ones at Disney World. The nurse at his doctor's office asked him, "Who said you could go to Disney World?"

We had been through so much; we were done asking permission. We were going.

Sitting together in front of Cinderella's castle, the princesses and their princes danced together and sang, "Dreams come true." I could feel tears prickling in the corners of my eyes; my dream was to be with my family, and we were all there together.

It was cool and pleasant in Orlando, in contrast to the chilly February winter of the Midwest. Nevertheless, our daughter and I came down with fevers. Brian, despite his weakened state, arranged for an in-room fridge, fetched antibiotics for her and cold medicine for me, and stayed with us until we were well enough to go back to the parks. We went to character dinings and rides and watched parades. We laughed at Crush's interactive antics during Turtle Talk at Epcot; his surfer-dude persona and friendly nature expanded beyond the animated movie.

We picked seats close to the stage for *Finding Nemo the Musical* at Disney's Animal Kingdom. The visual feast and music with the live-action puppets added a dimension of appreciation we previously didn't have for the story. On our way out of the theater, we stopped at a souvenir kiosk. Our daughter demanded a stuffed Crush.

"Why do you need another stuffed animal?" I asked, thinking of the at least 50 other stuffed animals in her bedroom at home, and the Minnie, Mickey, Donald and Daisy we had brought along for the trip.

"Because Squirt needs a daddy," she replied.

Well, how do you argue with logic like that? Of course Squirt needs his daddy.

The stuffed Crush quipped surfer language just like in Turtle Talk. Father and daughter mimicked Crush in hilarious one-liners that usually started with, "Dude!" My husband could only sing off-key, but the songs from the musical quickly became favorites. "Just keep swimming," Dorie sings, and we did even after we found out, one month later, Brian had relapsed for a third time. "Go with the flow," Crush sang. It became Brian's motto.

He passed away the day before our daughter's fifth birthday. Last year, she celebrated her tenth. I felt a lump in my throat thinking how she has now lived longer without her dad than the time we did have together.

I didn't realize, until near the end, how beautiful and fragile our perfect family was. Brian was an amazing husband and an incredible father. He is no longer here to put his arms around us. But he is still here. He is in our daughter, our princess, who is brave, confident and happy. The lessons he taught both of us remain. Each challenge we face, we face together with Brian's words in his best Crush impression ringing in our ears: "Go with the flow."

The National At-Home Dad Network's Brian Dickson Memorial Scholarship is a scholarship fund to help stay-at-home dads who would like to attend the Annual At-Home Dads Convention but cannot because of financial reasons. More information on the criteria for the scholarship and how to donate to the scholarship fund can be found at www.AtHomeDad.org.

PART SIX

FATHERHOOD IS NOT A PERFECT SCIENCE

"My son was okay, but I was not. I kept thinking I was a bad
father and that maybe I wasn't cut out to be a dad."
- *Mike Andrews Jr, father of four in Somerset, NJ*

I MADE HIM FEAR ME

Christopher T. VanDijk, Denver, CO

I had become a horrible parent.

Up to this point, parenting had been the easiest job I'd ever had. My wife and I were champs. We were (are) attachment parents; co-slept and never felt tired; managed to navigate New York, Paris, Amsterdam and every place in between without a stroller until, at two years old, our son was simply too big to put into his carrier. We did the Baby Led Weaning thing and decided if French Kids Eat Everything, so would he.

We were Zen parents.

It was a gas and it was easy.

Was.

After twelve years of us living in New York City, the opportunity presented itself to move to Denver, Colorado where our toddler son, whom I affectionately call "Turtle," could grow up near grandparents, aunts, uncles, and cousins.

He could have space.

We knew leaving New York would mean certain experiences would no longer be available to him, but a whole new array of opportunities would present themselves.

We embraced the gypsy existence, packed up all of our belongings, placed them in storage, lived with family, and began building our dream home; a reality we could never have afforded in New York City.

Despite all these positive things, I felt adrift.

I had spent the previous twelve years struggling as an actor. I was starting to earn a small amount of recognition as a screenwriter but it wasn't paying me the big bucks yet. When my wife and I decided I should be the one to stay home, it made sense. I was proud of my role and even carried around business cards identifying me as "Turtle's Dad." I joined the New York City Dads Group. I wrote a blog which garnered a tiny bit of attention. I also wrote for the largest Internet newspaper in the world which garnered, well, about the same amount of attention. But, I was finding my voice as a parent. One of the things I wrote was:

"I don't ever want my child to be afraid of me."

After our move to Denver, however, I started to become the parent I told others not to be in my blog posts. I had a short temper with my child. I stressed about the new home, the frustrations of potty training, my lack of career opportunities, the pressure to start over from scratch in a new town thousands of miles from the community I relied upon when times got tough. I stormed around the house, boomed and bellowed more often than I should have. I channeled all my frustrations at the only person in the room: my son. I don't even remember the circumstances surrounding my rants.

Except one.

We had been living in our brand new home for less than one week when my son peed in the heating duct in our bathroom.

He thought it would be easier to reach than the toilet. In the mind of a three-year-old, it made perfect sense.

I lost my mind. I didn't hit him - that's not in my make-up - but I did something worse: I made him fear me. I raged, grabbing him and pulling him into his room. I yelled at him. I don't remember what exactly I said, but I'm sure the words were hurtful and accusatory.

I ran back to the bathroom, ripped the vent off and began trying to work my hand into the flexible duct to sop up the urine. The metal cut and tore at me. I ended up with some pretty nasty gashes on my hands and forearms as I frantically tried to clean it up. I sprayed some kid and pet cleaner down there to neutralize and eat away at any urine left in the duct. By the time I went back to talk to my son, I had managed to calm myself somewhat. I stood in his doorway, arm bleeding, face red, lungs still heaving. He stared at me and asked if I cut myself. I grunted, "I'm fine," then breathed, "Get dressed."

My son started a very strange habit after that. He started asking us if we were happy – as if it were a problem for him to solve.

I was troubled by this, but didn't know quite what to do and, cluelessly, thought it was a phase.

A couple weeks later, I heard a yell coming from the bathroom.

"Daddy! Save me!"

My son had fallen backwards into the toilet, grasping both sides to keep himself from falling further. A solid stream of urine arced across the room, splashing everywhere. He called for me.

"Save me!"

I held his arms as the pee kept coming. When it stopped, I carefully pulled him out, took off his wet clothes, reassured him everything would be just fine and told him to go get new, dry clothes while I cleaned up.

He hugged me and then asked, "Did it get in the vent?"

"What?"

He began to cry and pointed to a spot near the puddle of pee, the heating vent.

In the middle of one of the most frightening experiences of his short life, his concern was that I might be upset about pee in the heating vent.

I had become so concerned with my own crap; stewing in the detritus of my unfulfilled dreams and petty apprehensions of this new life, that I forgot who I am.

I am Turtle's dad.

I'm his hero and the model he will emulate.

So, I put the last year behind me, this aberration, and began taking the opportunity to once again make parenting easy.

I wanted to create a better paradigm for him: open, vulnerable, strong, present, compassionate, kind and understanding, especially when it is most difficult.

In the theatre we like to say "acting is a moment-to-moment exercise." I like to take this further and say LIFE is a moment-to-moment exercise. I've had to stop, reassess, and find a way to be present in the moment, in each moment. I have rid myself of what Stephen King called the "Bad Gunky." It's toxic, it's contagious, and it's as easy to get rid of as it is to acquire. You have to get up every morning, look yourself hard in the mirror, release yourself from whatever happened the day before and look toward the future with wonder, greet every person (especially the young ones) with patience and respect, and simply be present in the moment.

This incident has helped remind me to look at time with my child as an opportunity to mold a fabulous adult and that every action I take, every word I say, is part of the foundation of his education for what it means to be a human being. Every day, I work at practicing patience and respect.

As a result, parenting has become fun and easy again.

THE CANOE

Chris Bernholdt, Devon, PA

It was a lesson I will never forget.

I had just started being a stay-at-home dad in June of 2008. We had moved to a new neighborhood, my wife was starting a new job, and my kids were young: ages three and one. I felt this undeniable urge to be the best dad I could possibly be since being dad was now my full-time job. I wanted to prove it to everyone, including myself.

The first week I stayed at home with my kids, my son fell off his chair and broke his collarbone. I was deflated, demoralized. I felt like I might not be able to succeed as a full-time caregiver.

A few weeks later, we went to visit some of my wife's friends from college. One of their parents had a cottage on Thousand Islands Lake in Canada. I had never been there and was excited about the trip. I was also determined to make sure my son had a great time by creating a memory that would wipe out our rough first week together.

I saw a canoe and asked my wife if she thought it would be a good idea to take our son out in it while the baby was napping in the cabin with our friends. She agreed and the three of us climbed into the canoe. My wife and I did well paddling around the island but once we left the shelter of the protected dock area, the wind wreaked havoc on us. Working together, we managed to get back safely to the dock. Then I said something I would soon regret.

There was pure joy on the face of my son. I did not want it to slacken. I did not want to add any more disappointment to his life. I asked: "Want to go again?" "Again! Again!" my son screamed. My wife said, "You're crazy. It's much too windy, but you can go yourself if you want." I'm a strong, six-foot six-inch dad, so I did. I wanted to create an extra special moment with my boy. I wanted to prove to myself I was not a failure as a father.

I headed out with a little apprehension, but confident I could handle the canoe by myself. I told myself this was a time to really bond with my son and leave a mark he would never forget. I did leave my mark but for all the wrong reasons.

Out in the open water, I couldn't control the canoe by myself. I fought the wind until my muscles ached. I paddled more thinking I had to make it back for the safety of my son. Thank God we were both wearing life jackets. The wind was so strong that I lost my balance and flipped the canoe. I grabbed my son as we both plunged into the frigid water. As a camp counselor years earlier, I remembered practicing swamping a canoe so I knew what to do. I righted the canoe and heaved him inside it. I knew if I tried to get back in the canoe, my lanky frame would cause it to flip over again so I put both arms on either side of him while I hung on the outside of the canoe.

I was scared. I knew if I was scared he was probably terrified. As he shivered and cried, I told him everything would be alright and soon mommy would figure out we were gone too long and send someone to rescue us. I prayed to God someone would come, soon. I held on tight to the canoe with every minute draining the strength I had left in my arms. A lump still forms in my throat any time I think about it.

After what seemed like a lifetime, a speedboat with our friends arrived and fished us out of the icy water. I hung my head in shame all the way back to the dock.

I learned a hard and important lesson. I learned not to force moments. Parenting is a journey. There are ups and downs. The proof that I was a good dad was already there. The bonding with my children I so desperately wanted would come in time.

I no longer force my relationship with my son. I let it happen naturally. Every once in a while, he will remind me of the day I flipped the canoe and we fell in the water and we will have a little laugh about it.

Bonding comes with time. Sometimes it's good times and sometimes it's bad. We made it through together, which is all that matters.

MAYBE IT WAS ME

Sam Owens, Omaha, NE

Sometimes things need to get worse before they get better.
At least that's how it was for my wife, Gina, and me as first-time parents. From very early on, we could tell that our oldest son, Max, was smart, capable, and full of energy. We also saw in him a firm resolve to have things his way. Yes, Gina and I were blessed, right out of the gates, with a strong-willed child. Very strong-willed.

At first we told ourselves his behavior was simply his age, or he was just a little rambunctious. We didn't realize it wasn't normal for every child to punch another child at a party, or climb out of his crib at age two, five to ten times per night. We were clearly having trouble controlling him from the get-go, but we were just waiting for that magical year when he would grow out of it.

Then came a wonderful and somewhat painful experience: Max's first parent-teacher conference at pre-school. Immediately when we started the conference, we could tell his teacher was nervous, almost like a doctor preparing to tell a patient he has a rare disease. She started off by telling us she loved Max, and that he was smart, and a wonderful boy. But then she went on to explain some of his strong-willed tendencies. He had trouble listening when he wanted something. When angry, he was almost impossible to control. This news was difficult to hear as parents.

At first, I was defensive. What did Max's pre-school teacher know about it? After all, he was only in pre-school! Surely, kids go through phases and grow out of it. Not a big deal. But then I started to internalize what she was saying. I realized she was trying to help us help Max. It was a hard thing to hear as parents; that something might be wrong with Max or our parenting style.

A few books and a couple of counseling sessions later, we realized what many parents realize; the problem was not Max, but his parents. We had been enabling his behavior through a lack of structure and discipline. Max, as a strong-willed boy, was not going to change his behavior without a darn good reason, and that reason needed to come from me, his father.

Whether it was a short-term phase or long-term problem, I realized I needed to be more accountable as a father and make immediate changes. This was a painful realization, but once I got through the initial pain, it was incredibly liberating. It gave me hope that I could put a plan in place to make improvements.

So I changed my behavior. I started setting up clear expectations for Max and clear consequences if those expectations were not met. There was a new Sheriff in Town, and he was going to have to get used to it. At first, it was downright exhausting for all of us. He would violate the rules twenty to thirty times a day and each time, he would get a time out. He would kick and scream and wail, but it didn't matter. We stayed firm and always followed through.

Before long, Max's behavior started improving. For the first time, he recognized me as a father and an authority figure which was probably a little uncomfortable for him at times, but also comforting. He learned he could always count on me to do what I said, even if he didn't like it in the short term. He learned to trust me.

Three years have passed since that wake up call in pre-school, and Max is thriving beyond our expectations. When I attended his second grade parent-teacher conference, his teacher expressed to us that Max is an obedient, good-natured boy. She told us also of his intelligence, which was great, but not nearly as great to us as the positive choices he is making.

It's never too late to adjust one's parenting style. My style with Max may not be the exact style everyone should use as a parent, but it worked for me. I had to change and adapt to be successful. I had to study and listen to good advice. I had to put my ego aside and do what was best for my son. It has definitely been worth it for both of us. Again, sometimes things must get worse before they get better. But they do get better. Much better.

USELESS MALE ANGER

Matthew Green, Los Osos, CA

My wife is a lawyer, and being a lawyer means conferences. Loads of conferences across the state, with lots of lawyers talking to other lawyers about lawyering. They would almost be fun to go to with her except we have kids now. One of them was still being breastfed, they weren't in school yet, everyone would miss everyone too much. That's what we told each other.

Hotels with really little kids suck. It's just like home except everything costs money, you have none of your tool bag to rely on, and everyone sleeps in the same room. Your girl needs a nap? Not going to do it in a hotel room, buddy. Need to change a diaper? Have fun on the floor. Want a single second to yourself? Not available at this time.

But we did it and tried to make the best of it. Strolling a baby around strange new places, I was always on the lookout for parks and places with food the kids might actually eat that didn't cost 30 dollars apiece like the hotels charged. All by myself, all day. Trying to meet up with my wife a couple times a day to feed and be together. Missing all the night stuff, of course. The dinners and cocktail parties and all the other activities that would have been full of lawyers and painful anyway, but nice to get out of the room and the baby bubble.

It always sounded so wonderful before we went. Tahoe? Hey, never been there, that sounds great. Palm Springs? Awesome, lots to do and I want to watch my Irish kids have heatstroke for three days. San Diego? Yes, I'd like to reserve four days of crying and complaining during the expensive and exhausting activities I'll be planning for the one and four-year-old. The pictures from the San Diego Zoo look nice though. Pictures never lie. Neither do they tell the truth.

By the end of every trip, the excitement had vanished, the room was trashed, and everyone was tired and cranky. Especially the kids. In San Diego, we had a nothing-in-the-hotel-is-good-to-eat-and-costs-50-dollars stay. So on the last morning, I jumped in the car early and found Noah's bagels (the best bagels on the West coast I had found so far, which really wasn't saying that much, but there you go). With bagel sandwiches in tow, ordered precisely as I was instructed by all the females getting ready back in the hotel room including the little one who could hardly talk but could place a food order to go like an old pro, I headed back to the hotel. The car smelled like salt bagels and ham and cheese and was the best breakfast I could think of for all of us. What a good dad I was, I told myself. Making a hard morning better, going out and enacting positive change for his family, braving rush-hour traffic and a long, annoying line of Southern California special orders on cell phones. Making my wife and kids happy. I was tired and it had been a hard trip but we were going to end it well. Have a nice breakfast, go to the pool, keep them from drowning, and then get back north where we belonged. Another little vacation saved from the brink of disaster by a well-made meal.

My wife was mostly made up and the girls were dressed by the time I got back with coffee drinks and hot chocolates and fruit cups and sandwiches all around. Grabbing her sandwich and mocha, my wife kissed everyone and hustled off to her day of conventional lawyering. I pulled the rest of the food out of the bag, unwrapping Sophie's and giving Lilah bites of the egg off the sandwich and fruit chunks out of the bowl. We slurped our sweet drinks and I cut up our sandwiches. Sophie took the daintiest of bites and put it back down with a disgusted look on her face.

"What's a matter?"

She looked at me with the pursed lips of a spoiled little girl who had tasted something that's just... not... quite... right.

"What?"

"I don't like it."

"What don't you like about it? It's exactly what you wanted. Egg, cheese, bacon, on a yummy soft bagel."

"It's got mayonnaise on it," she said and stuck out her tongue in nausea.

There was always something. Always goddamn something.

"Oh, Sophie. Geez, it's just a little bit. Here, I'll scrape it off," I said and took the little plastic knife to squeegee as much of the offending substance off as I could. Very nearly all of it. I reassembled the sandwich and gave it back to her. She looked at it with grave mistrust, tilting it open with a pincer of a tiny thumb and forefinger.

"It's still on there. I can see it."

We stood there, looking at each other. Like two arch-enemies at a stalemate.

"That's all we have to eat." I could have stopped there. Should have stopped there. But the anger was welling in me, mixed with my everyone's-gotta-eat-something pathology given directly to me by my Jewish half. I should've just walked away and left her to pick at what she wanted and eat more of something else later. But the male anger, Jewish worry, and the end of this crappy "vacation" got the better of me.

"So you're not going to eat it?" She shook her head. "So, what I just spent an hour searching for isn't good enough for you? Everything has to be just right, eh?" I said, picking up her sandwich. She just looked at me, unsure what was going to happen next.

As was I.

Until I threw the sandwich across the hotel room, onto the wall across from the beds. That felt good. Horrible but good. Then the other half, thrown a little harder this time, so the egg and cheese exploded, leaving a greasy shrapnel mark, the bagel slowly sliding down the wall. I grabbed the half of Lilah's that she wouldn't eat and the rest I sure wasn't going to touch as I yelled "THERE!" and then the room was silent except for the dropping sounds of breakfast on the carpet. Sophie started crying on the bed and Lilah giggled at the spectacle, not understanding anything but that it looked funny, all the food on the wall and floor. I went in the bathroom to attempt to calm down. I was like a low rent rock star who had just trashed his room. Except, it was like the opposite of a rock star. It was a sad day and breakfast sandwiches were on the wall and now there was another story that would never die.

Of course it was the first thing Sophie told my wife when we picked her up later. At my suggestion, of course. It was funny, eventually. Once I had calmed down and apologized then it was a story. My wife didn't seem as amused as we were now, checking out.

"Dammit Matt, are they going to charge the room for the damage?"

"No, I cleaned it all up. Mostly. There might be some grease marks on the wall."

"They better not... The room deposit..."

"Shut up before I hit you right in the face with a sandwich."

Sophie thought that was funny and so did my wife. After a minute. That old, useless male anger. What had I come to? Throwing breakfast sandwiches on the wall. A rock star without the money, drugs, or band. At least the children would never let me forget any of it. I could hang my ham sandwich on that.

SEEKING FORGIVENESS

Carl Wilke, University Place, WA

One Saturday morning, I was enjoying the relative quiet in the house, playing blocks on the floor with my baby while having a pleasant conversation with my 12-year-old daughter. This delightful scene was suddenly interrupted by my 14-year-old daughter deciding to practice piano. The sounds of her playing reverberated off the walls of the house making it impossible for my 12-year-old and I to carry on our conversation.

Upset, my 12-year-old yelled at her older sister to stop playing. My 14-year-old yelled back that she had to practice. I felt myself getting backed into a corner. The piano wasn't exactly portable, so we could have moved our conversation elsewhere. However, my 12-year-old felt the loudness of the piano was an intentional affront by her sister.

As the father of six children, this was nothing new to me. Siblings arguing and music playing all at the same time is the rule rather than the exception. For some reason, it was different this time. Maybe I was enjoying the rare quiet too much. Maybe I was enjoying the rare one-on-one conversation with my daughter. Maybe I finally snapped.

Whatever the reason, instead of simply moving the conversation to another room and keeping the peace, I spoke harshly to my daughter about her piano playing. I stomped up to her room and took away her phone for being rude and disrespectful. The peaceful Saturday morning had been shattered, replaced with a tension and uneasiness. One of my kids was crying in her bedroom and one was crying with me in the kitchen while I started to feed my baby breakfast.

As I was feeding my baby, I began to realize the depth of my parenting failure. I replayed the events in my mind, trying to justify my behavior so I wouldn't feel so bad about how I'd mishandled the conflict. Then my wife entered the kitchen. She had heard the commotion and spoke to our 14-year-old. I had royally screwed up. I had over-reacted and hurt my daughter's feelings, she told me. Even in my defensive state of mind, I recognized the truth; she was right.

I knew I needed to apologize to both of my kids for the way I had acted in response to their conflict. As a parent, I'm usually able to keep my cool and respond appropriately. In this instance, I failed and thus had failed them. I knew better. They deserved better.

Unfortunately, as a parent I make mistakes. When I do, I try to use it as an opportunity to grow as a parent and to model for my children how to apologize. This time was no different. I went to each child, explained how I was wrong and how I would handle this conflict in the future if it were to arise. Finally, I apologized and asked for forgiveness.

It was especially hard for me to talk to them when I could see in their eyes the hurt and pain I had caused. I felt awful. I felt like I had failed them as their father. They listened to my words and saw the love in my eyes I had for them. Thankfully, each of them forgave me and we moved on from it.

While seeking forgiveness is important, granting forgiveness is truly the key. I have taught my children to understand the valuable art of forgiveness. They did not have to forgive me. I was unreasonable and hurtful. Fortunately they knew it was important to forgive and knew I was truly sorry. Life, as I have taught them, is too precious to live in the land of UN-forgiveness.

DELUSIONS OF A STAY-AT-HOME DAD

Pat Jacobs, Elk Grove Village, IL

After many discussions, my wife and I decided I would become a stay-at-home dad when our son was 2-months-old. I was skeptical about whether I would thrive in my new position. Would it be enough daily stimulation, interaction, conflict, etc. to get my hard-working juices flowing?

At first, I looked at it like this: I won't have a real job. I'm taking the summer off! I'm going to spend some amazing time with my son. As the excitement rose for my new "job" as a stay-at-home dad, I decided to make a list of all the things I would get done:

- Read 3 books.
- Get back to my pre-baby weight.
- Ride my bike with the baby trailer up the big hill.
- Organize my photos in iPhoto.
- Misc jobs around the house: organize garage, organize office, etc.

At the end of the first week of staying at home, I had accomplished none of these things. I was beaten and broken like Humpty Dumpty after he fell off the wall. I was starting to gain weight and actually LOOK like Humpty Dumpty. Something wasn't working. My son napped very sporadically. Sometimes, it was 15 minutes before he was screaming and I had to hold him to get him to sleep. He couldn't roll over, crawl or do anything really except lay on his back for a short amount of time before he wanted to be held again.

I vowed to myself that the next week would be better. I would get him into a routine. He would sleep better. I would be a better homeowner. I would be a better husband. I would be the best dad. I would feel better about myself. I would get rid of stress, which would eliminate the growing number of grey hairs and reverse the trend of my balding head. I would get stuff DONE. So, I did the only thing any clear thinking new stay-at-home dad would do. I revised my list:

- Teach my son sign language
- Read 5 books (probably all at the same time)
- Learn how to trade stocks online
- Get back to my pre-baby weight
- Cook dinner every night
- Ride my bike with the baby trailer up the big hill (with ease)
- Organize ALL my photos in iPhoto
- Start an advice column for new parents
- MORE misc jobs around the house: organize garage, organize office, organize shed, organize crawl space, install soffits around entire house, fix the small part of the roof that was leaking, re-stain all the wood around windows, build a man-bookshelf downstairs, etc...

At the end of the second week, I resembled a mix of Robocop after the goons shot him up and Lard Ass from *Stand By Me*. I was lucky each day if I was able to get the dishwasher unloaded before my wife came home. My son broke me so badly that all the King's cookies and all the King's beer couldn't put me back together again. One day, my wife came home to find me on page 63 of my latest revised list where every task was, "All work and no play makes Pat want cookies."

Fortunately, I married an amazing woman who was able to bring me down from the wall. We looked at the constant changes in routine our son was going through and it made me realize I was putting too many expectations on myself. At that moment, the most important thing, the only thing, was to make sure our child was being cared for and loved. Keep him safe, fed and happy. I hugged my son, gave him an understanding kiss on the forehead, and I revised my list, again:

- Keep child alive
- Shower every day (or two)
- Keep child fed
- Shave at least every 3 days (or 4)
- Keep child clean
- Go outside every day
- Keep child alive

This list made more sense for this stage in my son's life. It was a list that wouldn't drive me into the Cuckoo's Nest, staring at walls repeating, "I'm tired. I'm tired." This was a list I was able to stick to and get things DONE. Like keeping the child alive.

Those first few weeks of staying at home with my son made me realize caring for him is a real job. It is not a vacation. I don't sit around playing games and working on projects. Eventually, there may be time for that. But the short and the long of it is this job is about helping my family at the expense of myself; helping The Wife and keeping the child alive. My son is two-months-old and will do a lot of pooping, crying and changing of habits. My job is to help him through all of it. Hopefully, we will get into routines. If/when we do, I can add things from my original list and start to tackle more of the stuff I want to get done. In the meantime, I need to enjoy this amazing opportunity to spend time with my son. I'm 30-something and I have waited for this moment all my life. If I don't take the time to enjoy it, it will be over before I know it.

Relax. Enjoy. And keep the child alive!

BAD HAIRCUT

David Kepley, Waxahachie, TX

After having children, the only thing my wife and I argued about was our financial situation. When we were both working, we were so tired that we never paid attention to what we were spending. This changed when I started staying home with the kids. With just one income, we had to prioritize our "life-style needs" to make ends meet. (I call it that because, "Every last enjoyable thing that we still falsely believe we can do and buy, even though we have two children," sounds desperate.) No longer could we crash exhaustedly into bed each night oblivious of spending habits. We had to wake up and tighten our belts. And when I say "we" I meant "me." Financial aspects of our family fell to me as one of my many other duties of being the at-home parent.

For us, the decision for me to stay at home was all about "what was best" for our kids. They did not need an iPad for every room, but we did want them to have actual chicken tenders instead of pink slime pressed into nuggets. As a result, things had to get tight around our house. Not the good "tight" like a Kid 'N' Play haircut, but the sad "eating cranberry sauce in July from last Thanksgiving because it's the only thing I have besides my children's food" kind. Groceries, lawn services, and wherever else I could find savings I did to keep our credit cards from overheating. One area I thought I could cut was our children's hair. Literally.

I informed my wife of my intentions and was understandably met with some resistance. I argued that I had learned to wire up lights in our home so cutting hair could not be that difficult. My wife countered that my comparison was terrible and said "affections" would be put on hiatus if I messed up her children's hair. A compelling argument and one I could not win.

Still, it nagged at me every time I took my boys to those "arcade" haircut places. Sure, their little faces glazed over when they sat perfectly still in the little metal cars staring at the TV, but my wife spent less at the salon than I did at those places… and they got bad haircuts! I figured I could save a lot of money if I took them to the cheapest place I could find. How could their haircuts get any worse? Murphy's Law loves to hear that.

We entered the strip mall hair cut factory and signed in. A kind older woman waved us over to her chair. She proceeded to hack at my children's hair only, in this instance, without the benefit of coma-inducing cartoons. When she finished with my second son's hair, she thanked me for being so patient on her first day. Her first day?! That would have been nice to know twenty minutes prior. Tufts of hair sprouted from my children's heads where they shouldn't. Empty patches resided everywhere like lunar craters. The entire decade of the 80's called to give their regards on what horrifying haircuts my children had. It reminded me of my fourth grade school picture where I decided to get a buzz cut and ended up being called "weed-wacker" (as in got my hair cut by a…) for a year. I think fourth grade me would have felt things were not so bad after seeing my children's hair.

As we left the strip mall, a grim thought hit me: these haircuts were so bad my wife would never believe I had not done them. I don't know about you, but I like "affections". I'm one of the last married men I know who gets to participate in "affections".

I panicked. I had nothing to lose.

I rushed home. There were tears, promises made, and bribes given. I got out my clippers and cut their violated hair. I completed the task, texted pictures to my wife, and received a "thumbs up" emoticon in reply. After she arrived home, I felt safe enough to tell her about the hair debacle and how I fixed it. She promptly alerted me that there was no hiatus on the horizon.

Later that evening, as I was getting ready for bed in front of the bathroom mirror, I had time to reflect on the day. "What a relief. There is something to be said about a job well done," I said to myself.

It's nice to be able to provide a useful service to your family. I always feel proud when I learn a new skill that can ease our financial burden. It made me so proud in fact that, as I continued to look in the mirror, I thought, "I bet I could cut my own hair…"

Sometimes it's good to stop while you are ahead. I was playing with house money after my children's precision haircuts. Then I blew it all by butchering my own hair and ended up on "affections" hiatus until it grew out enough to fix.

I learned another valuable lesson that day. Some places you can cut, other places you may want to compromise.

PLAYING CATCH

Owen Grayden, Brockport, NY

"Daddy, do you want to play catch?" my seven-year-old voice called to my dad as he fixed something in the shed. As he wiped the grease off his hands and reached for his glove, I could see frustration and guilt battling with one another inside of him.

Excitedly, I ran to the other end of the yard, turned and focused on his glove. I dug my left foot into the ground and, with one strong motion, I pulled the ball out of my glove, rotated my arm behind my right ear and fired it toward my father. The ball sailed through the air like a swallow. I was thrilled. I felt free! I felt alive! Then I watched as the ball crashed to the earth like a meteor, landing several feet in front of its intended target. My father flopped his arms to his side, bent over and picked up the ball. He yelled at me to release it higher and throw harder.

I gripped the ball with my stubby fingers, squinted at my dad's glove, wound up and threw with everything I could muster. The ball zipped high and true through the air only to fall, once again, at his feet. Again, I threw it toward him and again, it thumped to the ground. My dad became more tired and frustrated with me but wouldn't move toward me, acting as if he was an 80-year-old oak tree with roots 100 feet deep.

"Damnit boy, quit throwing like a sissy!" he yelled. He began to throw the ball back hard with an intention to cause pain which was his way of telling me to "man up." All I understood then was that it stung my hand. Tears came to my eyes. The excitement I had minutes before was gone. Now I was scared. My throws became worse. My father became more agitated. Finally, he threw up his hands in disgust and stomped back to the shed cursing at me under his breath. I felt like a failure. I hung my head. My shoulders slumped. When I picked up the ball, it felt as hard as the lump developing in my throat. Not only was our game of catch over, but I was sure his frustration with me would turn physical later on as it had many times before.

Fast-forward 30 years.

I was raking leaves when I looked over and saw my seven-year-old son holding a glove and a baseball. The weather forecast called for rain the next day and, with darkness approaching, I was in a hurry to finish. The hopeful look in his eye, however, diverted my attention.

"What've you got there?" I asked.

My interest in him brought a smile to his face.

"Daddy, can you play catch with me?"

"Sure," I said. "If you help me rake these leaves first."

He grabbed a rake with the determined grip of a pole-vaulter and set about collecting some of the leaves into the pile I was making. After a few vigorous minutes, most of the leaves were picked up. The yard didn't look as nice as I wanted, but it was good enough.

We grabbed our gloves. My son stood at one end of the yard and I stood at the other. He reared back and threw the ball towards my glove. It glided through the air like a swallow then fell to the earth like a meteor, landing several feet in front of its intended target. I picked the ball up, gave him some pointers and tossed it back. The next pitch and the one after both landed at my feet. I gave him a few more pointers.

As my back grew sore from bending over, I began to get frustrated. A muscle twitched in my cheek as a feeling of anger rose up in my chest. I wanted to yell at him and tell him to throw it right, to plant his foot down and use the power in his legs to get the ball to me.

As darkness invaded our evening, a memory came back to me. There I was again, standing across from my dad feeling small and insecure. I gripped the ball with my fingers. It was hard and I remembered the lump in my throat from when I was seven. I spun the ball around in my glove for a few seconds. Then, I looked up. I stared into my son's eyes. They were my eyes; eyes looking at his dad. Eyes excited to be playing catch with his dad.

I had a choice to make. I turned the outdoor light on and I smiled. I told my son he was getting better. I told my son my back was sore and he needed to get the ball up to my glove. I then uprooted myself and stepped closer to him. His next throw arced through the air and landed right into my glove.

After we were done, I told him I had fun and that I loved him.

My childhood memories are comprised of moments that echo the story of playing catch with my dad. I try not to dwell on the physical and emotional pain I experienced as a child but the repressed memories sometimes spring up and catch me off guard.

My father came from a long line of men who didn't know how to be a loving father, a line of men who took their own frustrations out on their kids. It stops with me.

No longer will I make any excuse for being negligent or for failing at fatherhood. My goal is for my son to have a different example of what a dad is and, with God's help, I'll be that example.

PART SEVEN

PROUD DADS

"I can't even stare at my son for too long without breaking down because of the joy I have of just seeing him living on this earth."
- *Tray Chaney, actor and father of 2 from Waldorf, MD*

NOT WHAT I EXPECTED

Wing Lam, Santa Ana, CA

When my son, Greg, became a teenager, his rebellious behavior and attitude between the ages of sixteen and nineteen was of great concern to me. Not only was I confused by his conduct but I also questioned my skills as a dad. I felt helpless. I felt like I had failed him in some way. It didn't stop me from trying to help him, though. I was compelled to not give up on being his dad.

I had heard the teenager years are often a struggle for both the child and the parents. Greg's behavior still came as a shock. He did well in school academically. He didn't cause any major problems outside the home but when he was home, he was moody, short-tempered and defiant. On a scale from one to ten for teenage angst, Greg was a seven. Nevertheless, my anxiety level as a dad, as well as my concern for Greg, was at an eleven on the parent anxiety scale.

Nothing I tried seemed to reverse his increasingly defiant behavior at home. I wondered how the sweet child I had raised could have turned into this irrational and insensible teenager.

Was there something I did to cause his lack of respect for me?

Was I not involved enough during his childhood years?

What was it I did or didn't do to make him so angry?

Despite my busy life and long work hours as one of the owners of Wahoo's Fish Taco, I felt I made time whenever I could to participate in his early childhood years. I worked hard to build a bond and connection with Greg through sports and other activities. I accompanied Greg to the YMCA Mommy and Me swim lessons where I was the only father in attendance. I also introduced Greg to activities like diving and tennis. By his mid-teens, however, Greg lost interest in sports, finding his passion in the arts and dancing.

When it came to dancing, Greg was a quick study. If a dance instructor demonstrated a routine, Greg had the ability and skill to imitate the dancing sequence immediately, not missing a beat. I quickly recognized his artistic talents and so did others. It made me proud that he found his passion and a love for something he enjoyed. After high school, he attended the University of California San Diego and majored in Visual Arts.

I hoped the time away at college would help. Maybe he was acting out because he wanted to assert his independence. Maybe he just needed a break from me. Whatever the reason, I thought it would give us the space we needed to eventually repair our relationship. It didn't. He became even more belligerent.

After his freshman year at UCSD, Greg asked me to pay for him to live in an apartment off campus instead of live with a roommate on campus. It was a lot more expensive so I refused. He was not happy. Then, during his sophomore year he asked me if he could transfer to New York University. His reasons were vague and the expense was unreasonable considering the fact that UCSD had similar programs and was in-state. Again, I refused to give him the money and again he was very angry with me.

Despite going away to college to follow his passion, Greg was still unhappy, defiant and disrespectful. I feared our relationship was ending like so many other fathers and sons who cannot get along into adulthood.

The moment it all changed came during a dinner he and I shared in San Diego when he was still nineteen. He was quiet but something seemed to be weighing on his mind. Finally, in a moment of courage or desperation or both, he said it.

"Dad, I am gay."

The first thing that came to my mind was: "I guess the wedding plans are going to change."

The next thing was a sigh of utter R-E-L-I-E-F!

Wow, the word "gay" explained everything! It relieved all the frustration and anxiety that had built up inside me. I was so happy to hear the word "gay".

Finally, everything from the past four years made sense. I understood Greg's behavior wasn't rebellious or disrespectful. He struggled to hide his sexuality from me and everyone else. He also was very concerned about how I would deal with it. But to me, all his actions and decisions now made sense. Now I understood why Greg requested his own apartment. When he explained his boyfriend Scott lived in New York, I realized why Greg wanted to transfer to NYU.

The reason for his disrespectful behavior turned out to have nothing to do with me. It was about Greg and a difficult burden he carried. While I was confused by and frustrated with his teenage behavior, he was dealing with a lot more in trying to understand his own sexuality. In hindsight, my life would have been less stressful if he had told me years earlier about his struggles and maybe his teen years would have been happier if I had known and could have helped him through it.

Coming out as gay, however, is not an easy thing to do, especially for a teenager. He was afraid of how others negatively view homosexuality. He was afraid of how I would react. He was afraid of the backlash I might receive from my customers if they knew my son was gay. I understood Greg's fears and was happy he came out of the closet when he did.

After dinner, I immediately went into acceptance and support mode. As the days, months and years passed, I became his biggest advocate. Our father-son relationship blossomed with each passing day. I also had the honor and pleasure of meeting Scott.

Greg and I talked on a regular basis about his talents, goals and dreams. I hooked him up with friends I knew in the music and art industry. One of them was Malcolm Campbell, the publisher of Spin Magazine in New York City. This new job afforded Greg the opportunity to be closer to Scott.

As I noted before, Greg was a quick study. He swiftly climbed his way up the fashion corporate ladder and made a name for himself. He built a good reputation as an innovative and upcoming entrepreneur. In 2010, Greg and Scott founded the company Kneon based in Marina Del Ray, California. Kneon is a self-service e-commerce platform that enables top-tier publishers to connect to retailers through any digital image.

Despite the turmoil during the teenage years, I wouldn't change a thing about how Greg and I have grown as father and son. I feel it was meant to be this way. Fatherhood has its challenges and you can't avoid the inevitable teenage years. What is important is how you work through the challenges and develop a relationship built on respect, trust, honesty and courage.

On that memorable evening at dinner, Greg gave me the best gifts he has ever given me. He respected my role as his dad; he trusted me enough to tell me he was gay; he was honest with me about his sexuality; and he demonstrated great courage by coming out of the closet.

While I feel proud to be Greg's dad, I'm much more proud of him.

OVER THE MOON

Lorne Jaffe, Douglaston, NY

Her utter excitement and bewilderment swept through me like nothing I'd ever experienced; the first time where I truly felt the power of watching the world through my daughter's eyes. It was a crescent moon, the type of moon that, in the immortal words of Cookie Monster, "looks like a cookie, but you can't eat [it]." In my arms, Sienna stared at the sky, eyes wide, mouth agape. She pointed.

"MOON!!!!!"

Her rush of joy filled me. Sienna had been saying "moon" for some time now because she has a toy that lights up and spreads a starry sky across her bedroom ceiling. My wife, Elaine, and I spent time in her darkened room with those electric stars and crescent moon teaching her words. This was the first time I could remember her recognizing the celestial body and calling its name.

The moon disappeared behind some fast-moving clouds. "Where'd it go?" Sienna asked, arms outstretched, palms up, questioning. I assured her it was still there. We waited until it reappeared.

"MOON!!!!!"

I felt so lucky to have witnessed something so wonderful, a parent watching a child's recognition of Earth's natural satellite, an occurrence that's been going on since the beginning of human existence. In that moment, I felt no fear. The heaviness of failure I'd applied to myself because I am a stay-at-home dad was further than the moon from Earth. It was so special that it made me realize how quickly Sienna's language skills are developing. How, because I'm a stay-at-home dad, I'm fortunate enough to enjoy childhood leaps and bounds that generations of men could never experience. I feel like I can see Sienna's mind and personality flourish, the gears turning behind her eyes. I'm head over heels for my daughter, even if I need a break from her quite a bit.

186

My one regret is that Elaine wasn't there to share the moment with me; my family was incomplete. Because she's currently the breadwinner, she does miss out on certain things, and I know she's devastated by it. But she's an incredible mom and when she's home with Sienna, the love between them is palpable. When she's at home, Sienna runs to her, so excited to see Mommy.

I never thought I'd have a girlfriend, let alone a wife and a daughter. My brain still fights me when it comes to having it all. My view of success remains warped. I still feel like I'm depriving Sienna by not taking her to a different museum or park or class every day, but I do feel enriched when we're home together singing the old "Batman" theme while she pumps her arms up and down, Batman in one hand, Joker in the other.

It's been thought forever that the moon has special powers. I've never believed it, but that night proved me wrong.

"MOON!!!!!"

My body is still shivering with child-like wonder.

MY DADDY LOVES ME

Keith Zafren, Nicholasville, KY

from *How to Be a Great Dad - No Matter What Kind of Father You Had* Copyright 2013 Peak Communications and Publishing. Reprinted with permission.

When my oldest son, JD, turned four-years-old, I took him to a San Francisco Giants baseball game. He had just begun to like baseball and I taught him in our driveway to catch and throw. He also had a growing fascination with trains. We lived within a long walk of the Diridon train station in San José, and the train stopped at the north end of the line just blocks from the Giants' stadium in San Francisco. It was a perfect setup. For JD's birthday, we rode the train all the way to the city together and walked hand in hand to the ballpark, carrying our gloves so we could catch the elusive foul ball. I purchased matching Giants t-shirts and hats for us to wear. We ate all the snacks we brought with us in our blue canvas backpack while we watched the game. It was a beautiful, sunny day and the stadium was packed.

On the way home, we played catch on the train in our seats that faced each other on the second level. We talked about the game the whole way home as JD imitated the pitcher and the batters. Lots of people on the train smiled at me, nodding their heads in enjoyment of us, and many commented how happy JD seemed and how lucky I was. What a great day—seven hours of trains, baseball, conversation, and affection. I must have told JD twenty-five times how much I loved him, how much I loved being his dad, and how much fun I had all alone with him. By this time, his two younger brothers had been born and we were busy.

A couple weeks later, I repaired a dripping sink in our master bathroom. I needed new O-rings. There was an Orchard Supply Hardware near our house. I once heard that taking one of your kids along when you run out on errands is an easy way to spend some one-on-one time together. This time, I took JD. I strapped him into his booster seat in the back of Mom's Champagne-colored Durango, and off we went. We were about a mile from the house when I happened to look in the rear view mirror. I noticed JD wore his Giants t-shirt and hat that day. I read somewhere that verbally reinforcing memories was a good thing to do with young children; a way of revisiting the experience to keep it alive in your child's mind. This seemed like a perfect opportunity to try it.

"Hey buddy, I see you have your Giants t-shirt and baseball cap on."

"Right, Dad."

"Who gave those to you?" I asked, pretending not to know.

"You did, Dad."

"I sure did. I love getting things for you and being with you, Son."

"I love being with you too, Dad."

"Do you know why I bought those for you?"

I expected him to say, "For my birthday getaway." Then I'd talk some about how great it was.

Instead he shot back, "Because you love me sooooo much."

I felt astonished. I thought, he's only four-years-old and he already knows the reason I buy him things and enjoy being with him is that I love him so much.

I had somehow been able, in just four years, to implant that knowing, that secure knowledge, in my son's soul. He knows and feels his dad loves him. I wish I had known that about my father at JD's age. As we drove to the hardware store, I still missed that feeling. I felt sad about the hole in my heart, the not knowing I've lived with all my life — the sense that my dad didn't love me. At the same time, I felt happy and fulfilled about the security my verbal affirmation produced in my son. I knew that was a gift that would last his lifetime.

My daddy loves me. There's nothing more important for a young girl or boy to know and feel.

PARENTING RACE

Anthony James, M.S., Fairfield Township, OH

O ne of the more salient aspects of my identity would be my role as a father to two beautiful, African American children. I have a son named Brendan, six, and a daughter named Tianna, eight. I consider being a father to them my main priority in this world. In my "other" job, I am a scholar of human development and family studies at the University of Missouri. A large portion of my scholarship involves understanding the role of race in parenting African American children and its effects on their developmental outcomes (e.g. well-being, self-esteem, academic achievement). Therefore, my partner (their mother) and I actively engage in conversations and actions that help us protect but also – in a safe way - prepare them for a world that may not always value who they are as human beings.

Through research and personal experience, it is clear that parenting race issues is at the forefront of the minds of many parents with African American children. The story I share in this volume reflects one of the prouder moments of how parenting race affirmed my actions as a father, and increased my confidence regarding parenting race.

My partner and I took our kids to the America I Am exhibit, which chronicles the history of African Americans, as well as their contributions to America. Given the lasting impact of our country's "origin sin" (i.e. slavery of Black persons), such initiatives have been commissioned to provide historical insight for African American and non-African American alike into what it means and has meant to be Black in America. My partner and I were somewhat apprehensive about exposing our little ones to the history of race relations in our country through such an explicit experience. However, we have already experienced subtle forms of racism and, while we want to protect our children, we also want to help them prepare for any future devastating events related to race and racism. As a father, this has been my goal since they were born, and this exhibit helped me with my goal of providing them the necessary tools of dealing with race-related issues in a responsible and healthy way.

While I truly enjoyed all of the exhibits, it was when we entered the replicas of the slave holding cells from the "Gold Coast" of Africa that the emotions within me began to stir. There was an actual door from the period and the solemn music, which included deep moans of agony by enslaved Africans, touched me at the deepest parts of my being. As I slowly walked through the exhibit with my daughter, I could feel the tears welling up in my eyes. My son, maybe from fear or just his explorative nature, decided to run to the next exhibit. His mother chased after him and I was left alone with my daughter. We slowly continued our sojourn through the exhibit. As I tried to make sense of what I was feeling and reflect on the pain of my ancestors, I could sense my daughter's curiosity and confusion. She slowly walked around the exhibit staring at the artifacts and trying to make sense of the writings and markings on the ancient pieces of paper and unfamiliar remnants of a time period that far exceeds her knowledge base. And then, it finally happened.

When we walked over to the final display in the exhibit, she looked up at me. With an expression that was the result of deep reflection, she remarked to me that things are better now because she and Jill* are best friends and Jill is white. That very moment not only created a wellspring of emotions for me, but also served as a source of confirmation that my parenting of race-related issues was working.

As an African American man, with African American children, one of my goals is to not only teach my children about the not so great things about our world (e.g. racism), but to also give them hope about the future. Through that experience, I am much more confident about "parenting race." The sensitive and appropriate messages I convey to my children have let them know progress on race relations has been made and, through the hard work of compassionate people, progress will continue. I am grateful, humbled, and proud of the fact my daughter has internalized that message. As an African American father, of African American children, very few things could make me prouder.

---

* Name changed to protect privacy

TUESDAYS WITH CHARLIE

Darren Mattock, East Lismore, New South Wales

From the time Charlie was six months of age, Tuesday nights have been father-son time. When he was 18 months, on 'our' night, I took him down to the river before sunset. We wandered over the rocks and down to the water's edge together. Charlie and I began throwing some rocks into the water; something I used to love doing as a boy. We stayed there until the sun went down, laughing, talking, playing, and bonding. It was simply magical.

From there, we walked over to a nearby Indian restaurant. Charlie and I shared a dinner of rice, curry and naan bread. He sat on my lap as we talked and shared our food. I had no idea what we were creating in that moment, nor did I realize an amazing ritual had begun.

The next Tuesday night, we did it again: played by the river then ate at the Indian restaurant. I could afford it since playing by the river was free and the Indian meal was affordable. Like the first Tuesday, it was a space of bonding and togetherness that was simply ours. I felt how much this meant to him, and it meant the world to me to be sharing this and creating this special moment with my son.

So I kept it up; every Tuesday night, without missing one. The first words Charlie put to our ritual were "throw rock" and "rice and curries." Sometimes he wanted to do this on other days, at other times, but he quickly came to understand this was a ritual set aside for our Tuesday nights.

When Charlie turned three, we held his birthday celebration at the same Indian restaurant. It was his favorite place. All of the family and extended family came to share this experience with Charlie on his special day. He beamed with delight and seemed so happy everyone loved "his place" so much.

The staff at the restaurant came to know us well. They were witnessing my son grow up and our father-son relationship evolve. We would always try to choose the same table (the one in front of the glass where we could stand and wave into the kitchen). They would always engage Charlie and give him positive attention. Soon, our order (we always shared the same meal) would be known as "Charlie's order." It always made my heart smile whenever I heard, in a strong Indian accent, "Charlie's order, please!" being called into the kitchen.

Spending time at the river and the restaurant with Charlie has been incredibly satisfying for both of us. Each visit had unique, precious father-son memories. From carrying him over the rocks in my arms against my chest, to watching him learn to throw rocks himself, to witnessing (with a mix of pride and hope) him walking over the rocks by himself, to the many, many moments of laughter, love and connection we have shared just being together.

Of course, it's never been the same as the magical first time we created our ritual but there has been some kind of father-son bonding magic every single Tuesday night.

These days, he dishes up the food for me. He delights in being "the provider" and even "the nurturer." I love that he has learned the art of generosity and the joy of sharing.

Tuesdays with Charlie have been the most rewarding and richest experiences of my life. I have had this relaxing, one-on-one opportunity to witness my son grow up while also developing the relationship and bond between us. I'm so grateful we have shared this ritual over these early years of his awesome little life.

I never conceived taking my son to throw rocks in the river and to an Indian restaurant every Tuesday night would end up being a prized jewel in my soul. But that's exactly what it is, and always will be.

AN UNEXPECTED DATE

Patrick Hoarty, Omaha, NE

I love Saturdays. Instead of everybody rushing about to get to school and work, we get to ease into the day: conversation with my wife is more leisurely, we make pancakes, drink coffee and read the paper as the kids (ages nine, seven, four, and 16 months) hop around the house abuzz with their play. On this particular Saturday, the kids called themselves "Fuzzles" and built a fort stretching from the living room into the dining room. The morning was spent back and forth between their project and helping me clean the upstairs bathrooms. My wife, Carrie, had her own project going refurbishing dresser drawers.

I was just getting lunch ready, something quick and easy because we had plans to finish cleaning and get to the dressers while the little ones napped, when our oldest Grace asked us breathlessly, "Are you guys ready?" I hadn't seen her in a while, although I knew she had been working on something down in the basement and was running back and forth upstairs getting art supplies, tape, paper, etc. (She does this sort of thing a lot.)

"For what?" we asked.

"For your lunch date at my restaurant," she replied. "It's in the basement."

I wish I could say I felt gung-ho about this prospect but what came out of my mouth instead was a litany of reservations: "Hold on, honey, we're going to have to carry everything downstairs… there's going to be a mess." "I'm sorry Grace," my wife said. "We're going to have do it another time." We went back and forth for a minute, with my wife and I trying to explain why lunch needed to be at the kitchen table. Her eyes were hurt, and she said softly, "But I worked so hard on it – please?"

Whether it was her persistence or that last line tugging at our heartstrings, we gave in. We headed downstairs where a big sign greeted us at the landing, "Welcome to Grace's Place!" Quickly, we were escorted to our table, where menus were waiting. There were a multitude of options, organized by appetizers, meals, sides, desserts and drinks. We each settled on chicken nuggets for the main course with a fruit cup side dish. I was feeling a bit adventurous, so I decided to go for the peanut butter/honey roll up as well. Our drinks arrived in plastic margarita glasses, transported carefully by our waiter James, seven, and waitress Rose, four. We clinked glasses and watched our youngest climb over the easy chair and settle in to play with toys near our table. Carrie and I smiled at each other, chuckling at the sounds of a hectic kitchen and a cook barking out orders to her staff. Soon the appetizer (peanuts) arrived, borne by James. Grace popped by to see how things were going. "These are great," we said. "Only usually, the waiter doesn't eat from the customers' table." "Oops… sorry," said James as he pulled his hand back from my plate (he does that sort of thing a lot). "He hasn't been through training yet," replied Grace.

Our main course arrived soon after. The wait staff were extremely attentive and even brought us silverware when we requested it. Somehow the dessert course was forgotten as the kids, er, staff, began the "entertainment" portion of the show with gymnastics. This ended abruptly after fighting ensued and time-outs were issued. The only one left to help with kitchen clean-up was the cook herself!

Looking back, I feel a bit ashamed it took such arm-twisting to engage me in such a wonderful experience. What was I thinking? I was so caught up in checking things off the list that I failed to see the most important things right in front of me. Certainly, we don't have to indulge our kids' every whim, but this was proof to me it's okay at times to relinquish control, to embrace their creative impulse (as inconvenient as it might seem at the time) to simply let go and run with it. Letting the kids guide at certain times allows them a needed sense of empowerment and ownership in the family. A trait I need to remember.

The overwhelming feeling I have from this day is one of intense gratitude. Moments like this make me grateful to be a husband and a father. I am grateful for the opportunity to witness the children working together, each with his/her own gifts, their creative spirits intertwining and making something bigger than themselves. They were so alive, so present in the activity at hand, so unconcerned about time. As a dad, I put so much time and energy into making sure their needs are met that it felt really gratifying to let them provide for us, and they seemed to delight in the opportunity to serve Mom and Dad. There is an incredibly intimate bond between parents and children – a love that is so visceral and so real. It is amazing how that love can grab you right out of the blue on a Saturday, unplanned, with food for your soul, no reservation required.

ONE MAN, ONE BABY, ONE VOTE

Brian Glaser, Maplewood, NJ

On the long list of things I want to teach my son is the importance of voting. Sure, it'll be a while before he's old enough to evaluate candidates and cast his vote, but in the ensuing years, I can try to communicate some of the reasons I think it's important to exercise one's franchise when the opportunity arises.

In fact, I've always thought of voting as a family activity. When I was young, my parents would take me to the local fire station on Election Day, bring me into the booth, let me help flip the switches, and then pull the lever that would cast their vote. Even before I knew who the candidates were or what a political party was, I had a pretty clear idea from my Mom and Dad this was an important thing we were doing together.

Those memories of early voting were from when I was a kid, not a baby like my son was on Election Day of 2010. Since you can't really explain any of the key tenets of democracy to a ten-month-old, I figured a good first step on the path to active citizenship would be to take him into the booth with me to help Dad vote.

So on November 2, 2010, I headed to my local polling place, strapped the kid into the Bjorn, and we voted together.

Because it was a big voting year (2010 being the Tea Party-fueled midterm Congressional election), there was a lot of tumult at town hall, with plenty of adults and even a few kids lined up at the machines. When my son and I got into the booth, however, we had a bit of a special moment together. The curtain closed behind us, and for a minute or so, it was just he and I doing something important together.

Having him strapped to my chest in the booth helped remind me why I was doing this in the first place. "Elections have consequences" is a line most recently attributed to President Obama, but it's been true for a long time. I know I can't personally turn the ship of state with my single vote but I do believe people showing up to vote, in numbers big and small, reminds politicians in local offices, the state government, the Capitol, and the White House, that we're here, we're taking part, and we've got our eye on them. Now the things they do will impact my son and his future, too, so I'm watching even closer.

My son and I faced the ballot of Congressional and local candidates, plus a ballot initiative or two. I was ready to make my picks. I took his still new hand in my somewhat older one and guided his little fingers to the buttons.

Sure, it may have been a minor violation of the strictest letter of the voting laws, but my son cast his first vote before the age of one, getting his tiny hands directly on the big levers of democracy. It was his first voting experience, and I plan to bring him with me every year until he's able to cast a vote on his own.

But for now, it's one man, one baby, one vote.

MAKING EVERY MOMENT COUNT

Don Mathis, San Antonio, TX

A divorced dad is usually ordered to be the non-custodial parent. Generally, this means he gets to share the first, third, and fifth weekends of each month with his kid - about 14 percent of the days per year. Yet time is all we really have with our offspring.

Some parents may have 100 percent, some 86 percent, and some 50 percent or less. But once the childhood years are gone, they're gone. Lucky is the mother or father who appreciates every day they can spend with their child.

I wanted to make every moment count. Even though, as the non-custodial parent, I had only 14 percent of the days per year with my son, I devoted 100 percent of my energies toward him in that time. It was the only way to make a difference.

I began bonding with him before birth. I brought my mouth to within inches of my then wife's belly. My deep voice resonated into the uterus and he responded with a kick or a punch.

Like most new fathers these days, I was present at the birth of my son. I realized something was wrong when the nurse said, "He's got beautiful feet." I looked over the curtain and saw she was right. One sole was smooth and one wrinkled.

But his feet were all I saw sticking out of the womb. Charlie was a transverse lie meaning he was coming out like Caesar. His head would be the last to leave the womb. I fought the urge to grab his beautiful feet and help the doctor pull him into the world.

Charlie's face was calm; his eyes clear and bright when I first saw him. They cut the umbilical cord and he howled like a teapot on a hot stove.

"Charlie," I called. Startled, he stopped crying and turned toward me. He recognized my voice from the countless times I talked to him in the womb.

I gently rubbed his side as he now dozed contentedly under the warm light. Then Charlie suddenly startled and he grabbed my hand with both arms.

And I fell in love!

This love has strengthened me, and him, in the years since. It has kept our bond strong even after his mother and I divorced; even after my son and I becoming every other weekend "visitors" to each other.

I've had to say bye-bye to that babbling baby, cheerio to a creeping crawler and toodleoo to my toddler. At age four, he could feed and dress himself and use words. Rather than just cuddling him or rubbing his back, I could now tell him how much he had crept into my heart.

"Where was I born?" he asked one day.

"Right here in San Antonio," I replied.

"No, where was I born?"

"At the Methodist Hospital."

"Mommy said I was born in her tummy."

"Yes, that's right."

"Mommy said only girls could have babies."

"Men can have babies too."

"Daddies can't have babies."

"Sure they can."

'But not in their tummy."

"No. In their heart."

"How did I get into her tummy?"

"Uhh… I put my heart next to her heart."

"And then you put me in her tummy?"

"Yes, that's right."

"Why?"

"Because we loved each other and we wanted a baby to love."

"So you had me?"

"Yes."

"You still love me?"

"Yes, I do. With all my heart!"

"I love you too!"

I made the most of the 14 percent time I had with Charlie and I gave it 100 percent. The first, third, and fifth weekends of each month, though, are not enough time to maintain a relationship. To help us stay connected, I wrote a poem about Charlie when he was three years old. He enjoyed it so much he memorized it so we were able to share a connection every night.

Though I'm not there to turn off the light,
To tuck you in and kiss you goodnight,
To read a book, or get you a drink,
It's you I love, and of you I think.
If you were here, I'd give you a squeeze,
And ask if you could give me one please.
So to the day we'd say our good-byes.
As we lay down and we close our eyes.

DON'T WORRY DAD

Christopher Lubbe, Overland Park, KS

This past year, I started a new job. This exciting step forward in my career created one major downside: I would no longer be able to drop my twin daughters off at the start of their school day before heading to work. I would need to drop them off at before-school care, over an hour before the start of the school day. This was a source of constant dread for me as the start date of my new position drew ever closer.

As the final days before switching jobs approached, I explained to my nine-year-old twin daughters how things would change in the morning. I shared my wish that I could continue our usual morning routine. They told me, "Don't worry, Dad. We'll be all right."

At first, I was relieved by their willingness to give this new situation a chance. But inside, I thought, "Don't worry? That's what I have been doing since before you were born!"

As I stood at my wife's side through a very traumatic pregnancy in which she endured seven hospitalizations and fourteen weeks of very strict bed rest, I felt helpless. I wondered if the babies would even live and if they did, would they be all right.

As I held them, in the NICU, feeling overwhelmed with joy, and fear, I wondered, how could these preemies develop to be all right?

As the physical therapist taught exercises to help the smaller one learn to crawl properly, I obsessed with how much further we had to go to close the preemie gap. Could I believe the developmental experts? Would they really be all right?

As I decided to stay home to care for them and then realized my only diaper-changing experience was a single instance with a niece (and I managed to put it on backwards), I doubted we would be all right. Was I even qualified to take care of these babies? I had no clue.

As I dropped them off at preschool for the first time, and they cried and cried (apparently the whole two and a half hours), I hoped both they and, especially their teacher, would be all right.

As my daughter, learning to ride her bike with me running behind, veered off the sidewalk and crashed full speed into a parked car, I was astonished both she and the car were all right.

As they went off the high dive for the first time, I questioned if the prepubescent boy posing as a lifeguard was doing more than watching his fellow female lifeguards. Would my girls be all right?

As they learned to make it across the monkey bars, I was excited for them and thought they were amazing! When a wrist was broken as a result of those monkey bars, my excitement turned to concern. Would she be all right?

As our tent folded up like a quesadilla on a camp out because I failed to stake down the majority of the tent, they were alright rolling with it.

When the dreaded day finally arrived and I had to drop them off at before-care, I still was filled with trepidation. The rush and hustle of an extra early morning routine, including packing lunches, helping with ponytails and remembering how to tie a tie, temporarily occupied my mind. As we pulled up to the school, my heart raced. I tried not to let my voice quiver. The girls were excited to see their friends and check out what they would be having for breakfast. They gave me quick hugs and I headed to the car. No tears.

As I exhaled, I thought back to their first day of preschool and a myriad of other major steps in their young lives. Once again, they had showed me, their always worried dad, that they would be alright.

Each milestone, from learning to take a bottle to earning a diploma, is a move towards independence. As a father, I hope and pray I have helped them prepare. I hope and pray they will be all right when I cannot be right next to them. I anticipate this pattern to continue throughout their lives: when they enter middle school and high school, when they begin dating, when they go off to college, when they obtain their first job, get married, have their own children.

And even someday when I die, I hope they can say, "Don't worry, Dad. We'll be alright."

SURPRISE ENDING

S. James Wheeler, South Lake Tahoe, CA

I've loved movies since the first time I saw one. For some kids, it's the candy and popcorn. For me, it is all about the surprise ending. Not all films have one, but when it's done right, a surprise ending can be the difference between a good film and an amazing one. While I seek out films with surprise endings, I try to avoid surprises in my daily life. In real life, it's better when things work out as planned. As a step-dad, I work extra hard to produce predictable endings. It doesn't always work.

I have three step-kids: two girls and a boy. From early on, my son struggled in school and was placed in special education classes. He was miserable. He worked extra hard to get into the regular classes. By his first year of high school, his test scores were high enough to make the transition. No more special ed! He'd finally made the cut, but his self-confidence was still shaky, defined by the years in special education.

He needed something to give him a sense of accomplishment — something he could get excited about. My wife and I went to work looking for ideas. He loved watching football and basketball with his biological father. Sports seemed like a logical place to start. Soccer was short-lived. Football was also a complete bust. Track and field was good for a few months. Basketball was quickly tossed aside. He gave up nearly as quickly as he started, explaining, "I'm no good at it."

At an early age, my son and I worked together in the kitchen. My mother taught all her boys to cook and I grew to enjoy it. I even considered becoming a chef. I let go of that dream, but always kept my love of cooking. My son eventually developed a mild interest in cooking, which gave me a great opportunity to draw him out and talk about his challenges. While dicing onions for an omelet, I'd explain, "Not even Shaquile O'Neil was a natural when he first started. It takes practice to become a good basketball player." While grilling chicken or making

Alfredo sauce, we'd talk about facing challenges and pushing through them. We discussed aching muscles from running track. We talked about why it's important not to quit when it gets tough. Although our talks didn't inspire him to stick with whichever sport we were talking about that week, the time in the kitchen gave us time to talk and bond.

Before he was done with high school, he had been in a school musical and joined his school's hip-hop dance crew. He performed on stage in front of hundreds of people. I saw his confidence grow doing things he enjoyed.

Our time in the kitchen paid off in a way I did not expect. It gave him confidence to do his community service work with the school's culinary program. He was a very good cook and by his junior year, he was showing me new recipes he'd learned in class. At one point during his senior year, my son came to me and said, "I want to get my degree in culinary arts and open a restaurant. It's what I love to do." My son was going to be a chef.

The economy was bad then and many adults couldn't find work, but he had job offers right out of high school. Ten days after graduation, he accepted a Line Cook position at a major hotel. They told him he was the youngest person ever hired for the position. He is currently enrolled at the local Junior College and will continue to work while he lays the groundwork for transfer to a culinary school.

My son has come a long way since his days in special education. He has worked hard to get ahead and took his own path. Sometimes, life gives you a surprise ending. Often, it's unexpected and unplanned for - but exciting!

THE PAIN OF DAD'S SUCCESS

Donald N.S. Unger, Worcester, MA

My kid finally left home.

I knew the empty nest was inevitable.

I understood the abstract idea of aging, and even illness and death, includes me too. But for a much-longer-than-adult period of time, I didn't allow my child's anticipated and expected solo flight into the world too far into my consciousness.

I remember my grandparents couldn't stop endlessly going on about: You will age; things change; got it.

As a dad thinking about things in the future - beyond the next diaper, the next pair of sneakers, the next family trip, graduation... was overwhelming.

For a longer-than-seems-survivable number of years, my daughter wouldn't let me sleep.

Sex for me and my wife? Too awkward to get into; let's just move on.

There was the driving, the meals, the vacations. The driving. The meals. The driving.

The driving. The driving. The driving.

There was the period where I made my daughter's life better. I felt like a Hero!

Then the period when I made her life miserable. I felt like a failure!

Then my daughter hated me, especially during the teenage years. It was a stage each parent must endure but those years felt like an eternity.

That's when I thought my life might be less stressful and happier if she hit the road. But, well... there are legal issues.

There was the terror in the high school years when I felt the most scared. The fear was deep, almost constant, bone-chilling, paralyzing. I couldn't ever quite catch my breath.

Women think men don't feel anything, that we don't notice, or we don't care.

I did feel. It hit me hard but I kept the fear down. Keeping the fear private was not about male ego or denial of feelings or keeping up a macho appearance. It served a purpose.

My now-gone daughter said to me recently that she'd wished she could have visibly upset me during her earlier years.

She hadn't seen the pain. She wanted to see my sensitive side.

I told her it had been there. She knows it still is.

I hadn't shared that part of how I really felt during those years. Dumping my anxiety onto her adolescence? How could that be anything but selfish and self-indulgent?

She was having a difficult enough time with her own personal stuff. I didn't think making my own fears and floundering more obvious would have made her feel better.

Then she left.

It's instinctive; it's primal. She wanted the freedom to explore the world, create her own adventure and make her own path. There are places she knows she wants to go. And then there is the unknown, the far horizon.

I knew she was not leaving because I did a poor job as a dad. I knew I had to put aside my own fears for her unknown and unknowable future.

Her departure meant success!

Success is the pain, the emptiness, in my house and in my chest, the vacant hollow freedom. I can be me again, whoever I might be now, even though I know fatherhood is forever. Her mother and I can be a couple again in a way we haven't had as much room for in twenty years.

Life without my daughter will be good… It will… It will… I slowly kept telling myself. Quietly repeating these words soothed the anxiety.

My daughter, who I nurtured and raised, is a part of me. But she is also an independent entity. I helped assemble a tool kit for her: values and life lessons, to try to guide her in the right direction.

Time for her to live her own life: navigate her own failures, struggles, triumphs and successes. My goal, after all, had been to help her reach this sharp, blood-drawing, objective.

Success is always bittersweet. I should… I will… I will… I will let myself feel both halves fully, just as I tried to teach her.

She leaves and I hurt.
There is also joy.
I am achingly proud.

CONCLUSION

Hogan Hilling, Orange, CA

A t a museum, two men stood in front of a Michelangelo painting, awestruck with admiration over the magnificent splendor of his creative artwork.

"Wow, what a beautiful painting!" one man exclaimed.

"Yes, it certainly is," said the other. "But it would have been more beautiful to have watched him paint it."

The completed project of any artwork, whether it is a painting, sculpture or book, is an achievement to be admired. While I feel proud about the finished product and publication of this book, I also feel extremely blessed, honored and awestruck to have been one of only two people - my co-author Al Watts being the second - to witness the dads craft the messages for what I consider to be a majestic piece of literary artwork about modern fatherhood.

I feel the dads painted an authentic portrait of modern fatherhood that embodies and represents all that is good, majestic and valuable about a father's role as a parent in today's world. Each dad poured their heart and soul into their story. Each dad used truth, tears and triumphs to highlight the true colors of modern fatherhood without losing an ounce of their masculinity. The end result is a positive, compassionate, sensitive, nurturing and endearing manly image of today's modern fatherhood.

The dads who shared the stories in this book demonstrated tremendous courage by publicly sharing their most intimate thoughts and experiences about being a father. What was even more admirable was the trust and faith all these dads had in Al and me. Most of the dads had never met us, yet they felt safe and comfortable enough to open their hearts and souls to us. I believe the reason they trusted us was because Al and I created a safe, non-judgmental environment to freely express how they sincerely and honestly felt about fatherhood.

What also impressed me about these dads was how they set their ego aside during the editing process. Most of these dads are not writers. Nevertheless, the dads rolled the dice and entrusted Al and I to nurture and craft their personal narratives about the challenges, shortcomings and successes they experienced as DADLY dads. Al and I critiqued and provided suggestions on how to improve the quality of their messages. Every dad whose story we had to edit for this book graciously accepted our input and suggestions.

In addition to submitting the stories, the dads also accepted our invitation to send us photos. The purpose of the photos was to feature each dad on the Dads Behaving DADLY Facebook page and our Twitter accounts to help promote this book project. At the time, I had no idea the impact these photos would have on the production of this book and on me.

After Justin Sachs, Publisher of Motivational Press, sent me samples for the design of the book cover, I asked if he would include four photos of the dads whose stories were in the book on the front cover instead of using stock photos. Justin graciously said, "Yes."

Along with the stories and photos, I received sincere, heartfelt words of appreciation from the dads for the opportunity Al and I gave them to participate in the book and publicly voice their honest feelings about fatherhood. I was overwhelmed with emotion to discover how grateful these dads felt about their contribution to the book.

Until Al emailed me the final manuscript, I had not read the book in its completed form. As I read the first few stories, I had the luxury of simultaneously putting a name and face with each story. It didn't take long for my emotions to get the best of me. I was so overwhelmed by their trust, faith and generosity in me that I cried.

Why the tears? I quickly realized they came from a place of pain and sadness, but mostly joy.

My tears of pain were for the generation of fathers before me, most of whom were stellar role models but were never given an opportunity to share their voice and, more importantly, receive the respect they deserved for their role as a parent. As a fatherhood advocate since 1992 and author of five fatherhood books, I have learned from my research that dads of past generations wanted to share their voice but feared people, especially their peers, would question their masculinity. They feared the criticism that would follow for the different way they parented and their views about parenthood. Furthermore, they were indoctrinated with the notion they should only play a specific role as a parent (breadwinner) and also didn't have access to the resource and support system available to today's generation of dads.

My sadness was for the dads who continue to struggle for the courage to speak up and let their voice be heard. I understand their reasons and resistance. I've been there before. One thing I learned from fellow dad Jim DiCenzo was if a dad would like a father-friendly environment, he needs to act like a friendly father, especially to other dads.

My pain and sadness, however, were quickly replaced with the intense joy I felt from the dads in this book. These dads are a prime example of the impact dads can have by speaking up and supporting each other for the common good of fatherhood. The dads in this book are a diverse group from various family dynamics, ethnicities, income levels, religions and cultures. Their actions speak louder than the words they shared in this book. All of these dads, in some way shape or form, advocate for fatherhood. They volunteer in their local community and serve as stellar fatherhood role models. Most of these dads also have never met each other. Therefore, their participation in this book exemplifies how dads can show their support for fellow dads even though they live miles apart from each other.

I feel extremely proud and immense joy to be associated with every one of these remarkable, insightful, dedicated, passionate and affectionate DADLY dads. I'm also thankful at how well they represent fatherhood in its purest and spiritual form. But more importantly, my joy comes from knowing these dads have proven the loving, tender, devoted, masculine spirit of fatherhood is alive and well!

CONTRIBUTORS

"I have a mug that actually verifies that I'm the world's best dad. That's a mug. That's not me talking. You can't just buy those."
- Stephen Colbert, father of three and host of The Colbert Report

All these dads and moms deserve a mug.
Or at least a tip of the hat.

Annette Acosta-Dickson is at-home dad Brian Dickson's widow and mother of their beloved daughter who inherited Dad's best traits and dimples. The perfect plan was for Brian to stay home until the squirt grew old enough to go to school, whereupon Brian would start his second career as a teacher and be home with her after school and on holidays. Unfortunately, cancer got in the way and Annette is now solo parenting. She promised Brian they would be okay, and though being a busy family physician was much easier with dad at home, the Dickson girls make it through with love, a lot of blessings, and the lesson learned to go with the flow. Read more at http://raisingdaddysgirl.blogspot.com.

Jeff Allanach is a dad of two children, Celeste and Gavin, and husband to wife of 16 years, Karen. The third of four children, Jeff grew up with a single mother in Gaithersburg, MD and vowed to play an active role in his children's lives. A professional writer and editor, Jeff also blogs in his spare time about his positive experiences as a father in hopes of encouraging other dads to also play an active role in the lives of their children. He and his family live in Frederick, Maryland.

Chris Bernholdt is a full-time stay-at-home dad of three kids aged eight, six, and three. He writes about his own adventures as the primary caregiver on his own blog, www.dadncharge.com. Chris is also the co-founder of The Philly Dads Group, offering support and socialization for dads in the Philadelphia area and is an active member of the National At-Home Dad Network where he is the blog editor. Chris' writing has been featured on sites like CNN iReport and The Good Men Project. When he is not writing, he enjoys the adventures of being a stay-at-home dad and capturing it with his photography.

Shannon Carpenter used to be able to lift 315 pounds. It was awesome. Then he graduated college and got a job. He soon decided kids were better than having nice things so he quit his job and has been a full time stay-at-home dad for the last six years. He once lifted the couch up to find a pacifier because those things are like gold. He continues to raise his three children and repair the damage they do to his walls. On occasion, he plays softball but his knees hurt after the game and he asks his wife why he got old. He likes tomatoes.

Scott Cathcart is a dad to two girls, Madison, ten, and Alyssa, eight. He and his wife have been married for 15 years. He received a Bachelor's Degree from Florida State University and is a vocal Red Sox fan. Scott is an Enrollment Counselor for Mid-America Christian University where he recruits and assists students looking for an online Christian education. He feels blessed to work from home, which maximizes his time with his girls. Scott has also been a team captain for his children's local elementary school's All Pro Dad chapter for the last five years. Scott and his family live in Wesley Chapel, Florida.

Tray Chaney is an actor who is best known for his role as "Poot" on the HBO's Original hit series *The Wire*. Tray made his first movie appearance in *Head of State* with Chris Rock and Bernie Mac, which was followed by a role in *The Salon* starring the highly acclaimed actress/producer Vivica A. Fox. Tray's newest venture includes stepping into the world of music as a writer, producer, and rapper. Tray's latest song, *Dedicated Father,* was inspired, in part, by the *Dads Behaving DADLY* book project. Watch the video and download the song for FREE at www.DadsBehavingDADLY.com. Tray and his family live in the Washington D.C. area.

Jim Chapa has been a stay-at-home dad for almost 20 years to two children. While he's not ready to claim victory just yet, the early results are looking good. A serial home renovator, he liked to call himself an "On Home Dad" during the early years. Jim lives with his family in the Chicago area.

Vincent Daly is the father of two amazing kids and husband to an incredible woman. A native New Yorker, Vincent is the Founder, Publisher and

Editor-in-Chief of www.CuteMonster.com, an entertainment website for modern parents. Vincent is also a digital media professional, artist, graphic designer, writer, and actor. He vaguely remembers normal sleeping patterns, although that well may be a delusion caused by lack of sleep. Vincent has written for USA Today, PBS Parents, The Huffington Post, The Good Men Project and various Video Game websites. You'll find him on twitter @CuteMonsterDad too

Jeffrey Davis is a former elementary school teacher (5th and 6th grade) now working as a full-time police dispatcher while taking care of his son Tommy during the day and going to class at night. He is pursuing a master's degree in school counseling. His wife is also a teacher. He finds being a dad simultaneously the most rewarding and the most challenging thing he's ever done. He plays bass, both electric and bass fiddle, been in punk, rock and bluegrass bands at various times since he was a teenager, enjoys hiking, camping and hunting and loves vintage cars. Jeff and his family live in Canyon, Texas.

Lisa Duggan is a writer, editor and entrepreneur whose passion and focus is the well-being of contemporary families. She is the founder and CEO of American Woman Publishing LLC, a media company dedicated to increasing the social and emotional health of today's families through online education, communities and publications. Lisa is also Associate Producer of the documentary film *Parents of the Revolution* by Dana Glazer about activist parents inside the Occupy Wall Street movement. Her writing can be found at TheMotherhoodBlog, The HuffingtonPost and Forbes.com, or you may read her very, very short stories on Twitter, as @motherhoodmag.

John Elous is a Canadian dad to a daughter, 11, and married to his wife for 15 years. He spent most of his adult life living and working in France, Mexico and the United States, but is repatriating to Canada in 2014. This involved dad looks forward to more time for running and playing tennis with his wife, and teaching his daughter to ski.

David Fetters is the dad of a beautiful daughter who manages to teach him every day more about what it means to be a dad. He enjoys being a dad and the many opportunities his daughter provides to explore life together. David and his family reside in Columbus, Ohio.

Joseph Fowler was a college football coach who decided to be the Director of Human Development and Domestic Engineering of the Fowler household, a.k.a. at-home dad. His daughter, Kennedy, was born in August 2009 and his son, Jefferson, in May 2011. He stays involved professionally with the National At-Home Dad Network. He and the kids can often be found at a library story time, the YMCA, the science museum, lunching in the park, or on the bike trail. Joseph and his family live in Bloomington, Indiana.

Brian Glaser is a writer, editor, journalist, husband and father in the New York metro area (okay, okay... the 'burbs). Brian started creating online content when it was still posted via a 9600-baud dial-up modem, and hasn't stopped since. Along the way, Brian has lived in big U.S. cities and the U.K.; performed in an improv comedy troupe; home-brewed beer; played drums and guitar; and amassed a record collection that needs its own room in the house. He hasn't lost his love of loud music, comic books or building forts, and is passing all of these along to his son. Brian and his wife and son live in Maplewood, New Jersey.

Andy Goldstein is a very proud husband to a wife who is out of his league and dad to two stellar boys in a league of their own. His time is spent reading, putting off starting his novel, playing drums, watching sports, and trying to figure out the best way to raise kids while remaining one himself. Find out more than you care to know about Andy via his blog, www.dadconteur.com. Andy and his family reside in Pegram, Tennessee.

Steven Grams is a dad to a four-year old girl and two-year old son and a loving husband to wife Stephanie. By day, he is tanned by office build-ing lights; by night, he is part mac and cheese chef, pillow, punching bag, Crayola artist, and storyteller. Read more about his adventures at www.dadtraveler.com, http://thetenyearadventure.wordpress.com and http://passportsandcocktails.com. Steve and his family live in La Vista, Nebraska.

Owen Grayden is a stay-at-home dad and desires to provide his children the benefits and blessings he always desired as a kid. Although failure happens, Owen awakes every day in the hopes of making it better than the day before.

Matthew Green is a freelance writer and has been a stay-at-home dad for the past 10 years in the Central Coast area of California. Raised in the Midwest, and a film editor in Boston and L.A in his past life, he escaped to spend his time chasing his two little girls and wondering what just happened. Matthew recently finished writing *The Luckiest Man in the World*, a humorous look at being a stay-at-home dad. His active blog can be found at www.worldsluckiestman.com.

Jason Greene is a former actor and playwright living in New York City who now focuses his time on being a stay-at-home dad. He writes about life and raising his 3 kids at www.OneGoodDad.com.

Ryan E. Hamilton is a father, blogger, podcaster, coder and Co-founder & Chief Web Developer of Life of Dad – The Social Network for Dads. He's also Senior Front-End Engineer for Verve Mobile, the pioneering leader in location-based mobile advertising. Ryan is Co-host of "The Life of Dad After Show" podcast with Art Eddy and is currently promoting a new blogging/podcasting effort - called "DaddyDev" - to teach his 7-year-old son (and children and parents worldwide) how to code. As a social entrepreneur, Ryan is devoted to both business and philanthropy and is dedicated to bringing about positive change in America, around the world, and around the universe.

Jeff Hay is a Canadian writer, speaker, parenting coach, and father of four. When he is not playing his favourite role of "DAD," Jeff is speaking throughout Canada as a popular parenting educator, working on his website www.thedadvibe.com and writing his parenting book for dads, *Wait Till Your Father Gets Home!* Jeff dedicates his life's work to improving the well-being of children by increasing the proportion of children growing up with involved, responsible, and committed fathers.

Mike Heenan is a doting dad of two daughters and a devoted husband of one superhuman Mrs. Heenan. An author, and Chief Content Creator at www.AtHomeDadMatters.com, Mike relishes the opportunity to be a stay-at-home-dad and, together with his girls, never misses a moment of this crazy little thing called life. Mike and his family live in San Mateo, CA.

Patrick Hoarty is a dad of four children. He and his wife are also fostering children through the state of Nebraska. Before becoming a stay-at-home dad, Patrick was a religious studies teacher at a Catholic High School. Aside from doing his best to keep up with all of the kids and a newborn, Patrick is the co-organizer of the Omaha Dads Group.

Dan Indante is a bitter, vindictive attorney beholden to two kids and a wife. In his latest book, *The Complete A**hole Dad*, 40-plus-year-old, fat, balding, unrepentant Dan pretends to be a model parent during PTA meetings and Little League games while secretly writing hateful screeds which rage against the banality of modern parenting. Dan lives and works in Beverly Hills until the creditors from his various real estate projects catch up to him.

Don Jackson is a dad of a 3-year-old and the stepdad of an 8-year-old. He writes about life, the universe and everything from parenting greatness and epic fails in the ever-changing story of fatherhood at www.daddynewbie.com. Don enjoys frequent trips with his family to parks, museums, and the great outdoors. He also frequently connects with fellow bloggers from around the world to learn from and network with them. Don and his family live in Albuquerque, NM.

Pat Jacobs has been a stay-at-home dad for a year to his one-year-old son. He lives in the Chicago area with his amazingly talented and extremely supportive wife. Pat managed restaurants and it took up the majority of his time with late phone calls, emails and texts. When their baby was born, they wanted nothing to stand in the way of their new family and decided he would stay home with the baby. During nap time, he co-manages the www.JustaDad247.com blog to help stay-at-home dads find resources, humor, and support throughout their days. The Beatles are the soundtrack of his life and his son has been a Beatles fan since the second trimester.

Lorne Jaffe is a stay-at-home dad who resides in Queens, NY. He is battling depression and anxiety while being the primary caregiver to his daughter, Sienna. His English and Media Studies background as well as his aspirations to be a writer enable us to listen in on his thoughts about parenting and life.

Anthony James is an Assistant Professor in the Department of Family Studies and Social Work at Miami University (OH). His scholarly work uses an interdisciplinary approach to understanding social interactions and human development, with an expertise in positive youth development, religion and spirituality, diverse family systems, and family processes. Dr. James is a certified relationship assessment facilitator through the PREPARE/ENRICH program and a certified family life educator through the National Council on Family Relations.

Eric Jefferson is a full time stay-at-home dad of two and is happily married to his best friend. As an at-home father, Eric has pursued his dream of being a writer and has been featured at the Huffington Post, Good Men Project, National At-Home Dad Network, and writes for his own page www.DadOnTheRun.com. Before becoming a father, Eric was the Vice-President of Operations with a private investigative firm, which means his kids have no chance during a game of hide-and-seek.

Stephen Kane started www.TheDadTrade.com, a blog by, and for, Dads in 2010. He writes about his experiences being a father to his son Avery. The stories chronicle the day-to-day interactions with Avery, ranging from the highs of a great sports day to the angst of math homework. Stephen grew up in New York, one of four children in a lower middle-class family. For the past 28 years, Stephen has worked at a ticketing brokerage in New York and has recently started a bookkeeping service. While the days are filled with working and family responsibilities, his proudest accomplishment by far has been being a dad.

David Kepley has been a full time stay-at-home dad of two young boys for two years. He is married to his wonderful wife Leanne who he met on a train in downtown Chicago at 5 a.m. David has always had a passion for writing and he blogs at www.JustaDad247.com to do his part in helping stay-at-home dads find resources, humor, and support throughout their day. Before having children, David worked as a pediatric critical care paramedic and did some acting here and there. He and his family live in Waxahachie, TX.

James Kline is a dad to two children and husband to wife, Michele. James is the co–organizer for the Triangle Stay-At-Home Dad (TSAHD) group in Raleigh, North Carolina which promotes involved parenting and offers a community for over 250 stay-at-home dads. James also serves on the Board for the National At–Home Dad Network and will receive a 2014 People of Distinction Humanitarian Award as a representative for parenthood. When he is not doing these things, James is brewing his own beer, restoring cars or writing on his blog at www.apexdaddy.com. James and his family live near Raleigh, NC.

Wing Lam is a dad to his son, Greg. Wing is an owner of Wahoo's Fish Taco, a national restaurant chain. The Wahoo's story begins in 1988 when the three Wahoo's brothers, Wing, Ed and Mingo, combined their love of surf and food to create a restaurant with an eclectic Mexican/Brazilian/Asian menu and a Hawaiian north-shore vibe. Wing and his wife, Kelly, live in the Los Angeles area.

Shawn LaTourette is a dad to twin toddlers, a boy and girl, who he equally co-parents with his former partner. A native of the New York metro area, Shawn is an environmental lawyer, writer, and adventurer who offers advice and support to LGBTQ parents and others seeking that illusive balance between parenthood, career and self. Shawn lives in Highland Park, New Jersey.

J. Adam Lowe is a dad to three children and works in organizational development and education. He is also a frequent radio commentator. His wife, Rachel, is a school counselor. J. Adam and his family reside in Cleveland, TN.

Christopher Lubbe is a proud father of nine-year-old twin girls. After spending six years as a full-time stay-at-home dad, he re-entered the workforce in 2011 and works in the healthcare field in patient relations. He enjoys running, camping, working in his vegetable garden and spending time with his family. His dad is his role model for fatherhood. Christopher and his family live in Overland Park, KS.

Don Mathis is a dad to Charlie. He is a poet, concerned father and editor and publisher of "The Fourteen Percenter," a newsletter for non-custodial parents, at https://groups.yahoo.com/neo/groups/NCP-TX-Grayson/conversations/messages. His "little boy" just celebrated his 21st birthday but growth between father and son never stops. Though this Texas family resides hours apart, they always remain close to each other's heart.

Darren Mattock is an Australian-based dad, passionate DADvocate and founder of Becoming Dad, http://becomingdad.com.au/. His groundbreaking work is focused on engaging, educating and supporting expectant and new dads as they prepare for birth and the role of fatherhood. Darren has been a part-time stay-at-home dad to his young son Charlie for an awesome six years of life and embraces fatherhood as one of the greatest gifts of his life. He proudly acknowledges that

Charlie is his greatest source of inspiration. Darren and his family live in Byron Bay, Australia.

Kevin McKeever writes in between his duties as an at-home dad to a brood of three: boy, girl and canine. His newspaper columns for Hearst Connecticut Media Group won first place honors from the National Society of Newspaper Columnists in 2013. He also writes the "Dad About Town" column for *Stamford* magazine in Connecticut, plays editor for the City Dads Group (www.citydadsgroup.com), blogs at *Always Home and Uncool* (www.alwayshomeanduncool.com), and occasionally tricks businesses into hiring him as a copywriter. Kevin's work has been featured in Canada's *Globe and Mail*, the New York *Daily News* and landfills worldwide.

Jameson Mercier is a dad to three children, Asrielle, five, Tamar, three, and Jaeson, one, and husband to his lovely wife Herdyne. Jameson is a Licensed Clinical Social Worker in private practice. He is completing his doctorate degree in Marriage and Family Therapy at Nova Southeastern University in Davie. His research focuses on Afro-Caribbean fathers as primary caregivers. He is also an adjunct professor of social work at Broward College, Barry University, and Nova Southeastern University. Jameson and his family live in Fort Lauderdale, Florida.

Chris Middleton is a dad to two boys, Joshua, 12, and Daniel, 10, and husband to wife, Vicki. Being able to stay home with the boys has enabled him to have more free time on the weekends and be more involved with their lives. He also volunteers at the elementary school and started a committee in the PTA, called All Pro Dad's club. It was the first chapter of the Tony Dungy endorsed cause, www.allprodad.com, in his area. When his schedule allows, he manages and/or coaches both his son's travel baseball teams and substitute teaches at his sons' school. Chris and his family live in Oviedo, Florida.

Oren Miller was born in Israel, moved to London where he met an American woman, then moved to Baltimore with her. Oren is a stay-at-home dad to two boys. His blog, www.BloggerFather.com, features the voices of involved, active dads and has been featured on The Huffington Post, CNN, HLN, The Baltimore Sun, Scary Mommy, The Good Men Project, and Redbook. He is also the founder of the Dad Bloggers group on Facebook.

Sam Owens is the father of three children. When he is not being DADLY, he enjoys reading business books, playing basketball, and watching 80's movies. Sam was lucky to grow up in Walnut Creek, California, and he still enjoys a strong relationship with his dad who has taught him that being a dad continues your whole life. Sam and his family live in Omaha, NE.

John Pawlowski lives in Omaha, NE with his wife and three children where he works as a brand manager. Although he received his bachelor's degree at BYU and his MBA from Indiana University, his favorite title is "Daddy". Publishing an occasional story keeps his mind engaged, while participating in Tough Mudder events keeps him physically active. He is involved weekly with the youth organization at his church, and when he grows up, he'd like to teach a college course for fun.

Matt Peregoy is a graduate of Messiah College and lives outside Baltimore, MD with his wife and daughter. When he is not busy daddying, he enjoys gardening and making music. During his two year stint as a stay-at-home dad, he kept a blog called The Real Matt Daddy. You can still find his writing at therealmattdaddy.blogspot.com.

Ben Petrick is a husband to wife, Kellie, and a dad to two daughters. Ben was a former Major League Baseball Player for the Colorado Rockies and Detroit Tigers. After he retired at the age of 27, Ben publicly announced he had Parkinson's disease. Ben survived two brain surgeries and relishes his role as a dad. Ben is a celebrated author, recently publishing the acclaimed *40,000 to One*, a collection of stories about his journey. He is also founder of Faith In The Game, a blog containing written submissions by prominent athletes of faith. Ben and his family live in Hillsboro, Oregon.

Gerald Plummer is the dad to two sons and a husband to his wife for 20 years. He was born in Missouri, raised in a three-room "shotgun" house without running water and is a country boy at heart. He has been successful in many different industries; Chemist, College Instructor, actor, writer, director, producer of stage and TV, ran for California governor when Arnold ran, and most recently, construction project manager for multi-million dollar projects up and down the west coast. A couple more years of "tax deductions" and he and his wife will become empty-nesters. Gerald and his family live in Burbank, California.

Sean Rose is a dad to seven children. In addition to homeschooling his crew of Rosebuds, Sean and his wife, Lisa, work together to develop educational materials for hospitals, non-profit organizations, parochial schools and churches. He enjoys any reason to be outdoors and is most likely found with a fishing pole in his hand and a backpack (or in his case a Kelty child carrier) strapped to his back ready for a hike. Sean and Lisa reside in the farm country of Tennessee with their seven children: Jeffrey, Kassidy, Chloe, Sophia, Stella, Charlie, and little man, Salvatore.

Chris Routly has been a full-time stay-at-home dad since 2009, a role which he has embraced totally. Inspired by his experiences, he is the creator of The Daddy Doctrines (http://daddydoctrines.com), where he writes and draws about being a stay-at-home dad. His little blog got big attention when he joined others in the dad community in calling out some big brands who were still falling back on old stereotypes in their advertising, presenting fathers as inept parents. In addition to his blog, Chris has written and illustrated several of his own self-published children's books as SketchBoy Productions (http://sketchboyproductions.com).

Mike Sager is a stay-at-home dad to one daughter and expecting a new baby boy. He has an MBA, is an active Civil War re-enactor, Girl Scout leader, story teller, game designer, former CEO, and a damn fine cook. He sits on the board of directors of several charities and is known to put on beer, whiskey and wine tastings to raise money for his favorite causes.

Scotty Schrier is a stay-at-home dad of two boys. When he's not chasing the kids around, he's writing. He started www.DadsWhoChangeDiapers.com to help fill a need that many dads feel; the need to know where a dad-accessible changing station is located. He has one collection of short fiction published on Amazon for the Kindle, and recently finished a new novel which should be published soon. He and his wife have been together for 20 years and now live in Tampa with their boys. You can find him on Twitter as @DiaperDads.

Billy Stamey is a dad to a vivacious five-year-old little boy, Rohen James. Billy, his wife Nickey Rohen, and the family pets reside in a rural county of Western North Carolina within the Blue Ridge Mountains. Billy is a designer for a large national manufacturing corporation. When not coaching one of Rohen's sports teams, Billy can be found running or working outside in the family's large yard. Billy feels that raising a son is a commission from God and takes the role of "dad" very seriously.

Matt Swigart is a pastor who has served in youth, young adult and family ministry for almost 15 years. Matt's primary ministry function, however, is with his wonderful family: wife Christina and three amazing children, Caitlyn, ten, Caleb, seven, and Lucy, three. Along with local church and family ministry, Matt is the Head Men's and Women's Tennis Coach at the University of Northwestern-St. Paul where he gets to utilize his passion for discipleship, mentoring and coaching in a setting where he can use the game of tennis to disciple his players. Pastor Matt and his family live near St. Paul, MN.

Donald N.S. Unger is a dad to one daughter. He is also a New York City born writer and the author of *Men Can: The Changing Image & Reality of Fatherhood in America*, www.men-can.com.

Christopher T. VanDijk is an actor, writer, dad. Chris is an award-winning screenwriter and actor, having been awarded the 2012 CAPE New Writer's Award (Screenplay) and named a semifinalist for the coveted Nicholl Fellowship. He is a contributor to the Huffington Post and you can find him raising Cain online at his blog, http://SkinnedKneesInShortPants.blogspot.com. Chris is also the facilitator of the Denver Dad's Group. He can usually be found in local Denver parks chasing a toddler, digging for dinosaur bones, and discussing everything from politics to pasta.

Jason Ward is a husband to his wife of 17 years, Robin, and dad to son, Elijah. When Elijah started Kindergarten, Jason and Robin saw an opportunity to encourage fathers to be more engaged in the school by starting a "Dad's Club" which has grown to more than 120 members in three years (in a school of 450 students). Jason has a full team of great father role-models serving in leadership and volunteer roles. Jason and his family live in Benbrook, Texas.

S. James Wheeler is a dad to three stepchildren. Wheeler's research on the blended family dynamic has made him a well-known authority in the field of family dynamics research. He is a public speaker who advocates for step-dads and promotes parenting success. He has authored two books, *The Stepdad's Guide: Resolving Blended Family Conflict* and *Stepdad 101: What to Know BEFORE You Marry a Single Mom* and the founder of www.stepdadding.com, an informational and inspirational website for step-dads.

Carl Wilke is blessed to be father to six amazing children, ages 19, 14, 12, 9, 4 and 1, and a husband to his lovely wife for 21 years. He grew up in Wisconsin and taught elementary school for six years before becoming a full-time stay-at-home dad in 2000. Recently, he and his family moved to Washington State and have adopted the Seattle Seahawks as their second favorite team behind the Packers. He blogs at www.bigcheesedad.com when not playing sports and outdoor activities such as hiking, biking and kayaking with his kids. At 6'8" tall, Carl is likely the tallest SAHD in America!

Keith Zafren is a dad expert and coach who learned first-hand how to raise great kids and stay close to them, no matter what. He is an engaging speaker and writer who has touched thousands of lives with his book *How to Be a Great Dad—No Matter What Kind of Father You Had.* Learn more about how Keith helps dads become the dads you've always wanted to be at www.thegreatdadsproject.org. Keith and his family live in Nicholasville, Kentucky.

COMING SOON

FROM **MOTIVATIONAL PRESS** BY

HOGAN HILLING AND **AL WATTS**

Moms Speak Out on Dads Behaving DADLY: Truths, Tears and Triumphs from <u>Moms</u> on Modern Fatherhood

Dads Behaving DADLY 2: More Truths, Tears and Triumphs of Modern Fatherhood

If you are interested in submitting your DADLY story to our next books, please visit www.DadsBehavingDadly.com and follow us @ TheDadGuru and @BehavingDadly.

ALSO FROM HOGAN HILLING

When Divorce Do Us Part (Motivational Press, 2014)

Pacifi(her): What She's Thinking When She's Pregnant (Turner Publishing, 2011)

Rattled: What He's Thinking When You're Pregnant (Turner Publishing, 2011)

The Modern Mom's Guide to Dads (Cumberland House, 2007)

The Man Who Would Be Dad (Capital Books, 2002)

CPSIA information can be obtained
at www.ICGtesting.com
Printed in the USA
FFOW01n0339260614
6036FF